Twayne's English Authors Series

EDITOR OF THIS VOLUME

Arthur F. Kinney

University of Massachusetts, Amherst

Edmund Waller

TEAS 266

Edmund Waller

EDMUND WALLER

By JACK G. GILBERT

Louisiana State University

TWAYNE PUBLISHERS

A DIVISION OF G. K. HALL & CO., BOSTON

Copyright © 1979 by G K. Hall & Co.

Published in 1979 by Twayne Publishers,
A Division of G. K. Hall & Co.
All Rights Reserved

Printed on permanent/durable acid-free paper and bound in the
United States of America

First Printing

Library of Congress Cataloging in Publication Data

Gilbert, Jack Glenn.
Edmund Waller.

(Twayne's English authors series ; TEAS 266)
Bibliography: p. 152–56
Includes index.
1.   Waller, Edmund, 1606–1687.
2.   Poets, English—Early modern, 1500–1700—Biography.
PR3753.G5   821'.4   [B]   78-31322
ISBN 0-8057-6763-0

For C. B.

Contents

About the Author

The author is Professor of English at Louisiana State University, Baton Rouge. After receiving his doctorate in English at the University of Texas at Austin, he has taught at Louisiana State and has served there in a number of administrative positions: director of honors, associate dean of the College of Arts and Sciences, director of the LSU-Summer Program in London. Presently he is coordinator of foreign study programs. He is the author of a book on Jonathan Swift.

Preface

In his own day Edmund Waller established a reputation for himself in two careers. As a poet, he became a celebrity. As a member of the House of Commons, he attracted considerable if not always honorific attention. After his death and after the decline of his fame from its Augustan zenith, the notices focus more narrowly on two topics: a small group of lyric poems (which persevere in the anthologies) and his actions during the Long Parliament (especially the plot to which his name has been given). Recently several critics have done more justice to the range of his works; the lyrics have been examined afresh, and the political, panegyrical poems analyzed with care. I have found the criticism very helpful toward the primary goal of the present study, a discussion of Waller's most significant works: the poems generally accounted his best and some neglected fine pieces (a few lyrics, poems about art).

Chapter 1 deals with Waller's life, which is interesting in itself because of his involvement in affairs of state and because of his wide acquaintance among "the great." Some attention to his life is also unavoidable because estimates of his worth as a poet have been influenced by largely adverse judgments of his character. The next two chapters concern his major poems: Chapter 2, the lyrics, Chapter 3, the political poems (or panegyrics). Chapter 4 combines, as topics importantly related, Waller's view of art and the question of his place in English literature. An indirect goal throughout the book, and a direct one at the end, is to account for the high value the Augustans assigned to Waller's poetry.

I am grateful to several colleagues who have read this study and made valuable suggestions: Professors John I. Fischer, Don D. Moore, Herbert B. Rothschild, Jr., and Lawrence A. Sasek. I am pleasantly obligated to Dr. John V. Price of the University of Edinburgh for bibliographical advice and for the use, generously and hospitably allowed, of his personal library. Mr. Jacques Bagur's criticism of a number of points of argument has been especially useful. Dr. Margaret Deas Cohen, whose 1931

Cambridge dissertation is a basic study of Waller, kindly answered several queries and gave me permission to quote from her work. To Dr. Warren Chernaik I am obliged, not only for his valuable study of Waller, but also for generously helping me track down the Waller family papers.

I am grateful to the number of libraries and record offices: especially the British Library, the Bodleian Library, the National Library of Scotland, the House of Lords Record Office, the *Bibliothèque Nationale,* the Search Room of the Royal Commission on Historical Manuscripts, the Humanities Research Center of the University of Texas, the Buckinghamshire County Record Office, the Public Record Office, the Guildhall Library.

To the Research Council of the Graduate School of Louisiana State University in Baton Rouge, I am indebted for grants for research in England in 1972 and 1975. I am grateful to the University, through the friendly agency of Dean Irwin A. Berg, for support in the expenses of scholarship.

JACK G. GILBERT

Baton Rouge, Louisiana

Chronology

1606   Edmund Waller born March 3 at Coleshill (then in Hertfordshire, now in Buckinghamshire), the oldest son of Robert Waller and Anne Hampden Waller.

1616   Death of his father, who left him property with an income of about £2500 a year.

1620   Admitted fellow-commoner of King's College, Cambridge (apparently never taking a degree).

1624- Named to represent Ilchester, Somerset, in the fourth and
1625   last parliament of James I.

1625   Represented Chipping Wycombe, Buckingham, in the first parliament of Charles I.

1628- Represented Amersham (or Agmondesham), Bucking-
1629   ham, in the third parliament of Charles I.

1631   Eloped with a ward of the City of London, Anne Banks, an heiress; pardoned by the King.

1635   Anne Waller's death after giving birth to a second child.

1635?-Became a member of the brilliant circle of Lucius Cary,
1640? Viscount Falkland; his poems circulated in manuscript.

1636?-Courtship of Dorothy Sidney (Sacharissa); the period of
1639   his greatest lyrics, which were first published in 1645.

1640   Returned for Amersham to the Short Parliament.

1640   Represented St. Ives, Cornwall, in the Long Parliament, until disenabled in 1643.

1642   After some hesitation, remained in parliament when the King set up his standard at Nottingham, August 25.

1643   May 31, arrested by the leaders of parliament for coordinating a strategem by moderates ("Waller's Plot") to deliver London to the king.

1643   June and July, gave evidence to a Commons committee against his associates and himself.

1643   July 4, made a brilliant and abject defense of himself before the House of Commons; disenabled on July 14.

1643- In custody from May 31, in the Tower of London from the
1644 fall of 1643; banished and fined £10,000.

1642?-Married Mary Bresse.
1644?

1645- Banishment. Lived in several cities in France, traveled
1652 with John Evelyn through Italy, Switzerland, France in
1646.

1645 Publication of his poems in several issues (editions?), with
three of his speeches in some issues, perhaps all printings
without his authorization.

1651 Pardoned by act of parliament, probably on the recom-
mendation of Cromwell.

1652 Return to England.

1655 "A Panegyric to My Lord Protector," his best political
poem.

1660 "To the King Upon His Majesty's Happy Return."

1661 "On St. James's Park," his finest loco-descriptive poem.

1661- M. P. for Hastings, Cinque Ports.
1679

1664 *Poems, Etc.* "never till now corrected and published with
the approbation of the Author," and *Pompey the Great*, a
translation of Corneille's play (with others).

1666 "Instructions to a Painter," which occasioned several
parodies, one at least by Andrew Marvell.

1668 Third edition of collected poems: *Poems, Etc.*, containing
poems published or written after the 1664 edition.

1677 Death of Mary Bresse Waller.

1682 Fourth edition of *Poems, Etc.*

1685 *Divine Poems.*

1685- Either he or his son represented Saltash, Cornwall, in the
1687 first, and last, parliament of James II.

1686 *Poems, Etc.*, fifth edition, and the last supervised by
Waller himself.

1687 October 21, death of Waller.

1690 *The Second Part of Mr. Waller's Poems*, which includes
unpublished verse and his alterations of Beaumont and
Fletcher's *The Maid's Tragedy*.

CHAPTER 1

The Life of a "Happy" Poet

I Introduction

IN defense of his own optimistic mode of writing, Edmund Waller once said that "men write ill things well, and good things ill; that Satyricall writing was downe-hill, most easie and naturall; that at Billingsgate one might hear great heights of such witt; that the cursed earth naturally produces briars and thornes and weeds, but roses and fine flowers require cultivation."[1] To judge only from Waller's poems—from almost any couplet in his poems—he was a man able to cultivate "fine flowers," to look on the pleasant, the sunny, the good side of nearly everything. He encourages his biographers, his critics, and his readers to do the same.

There was much good in his life. He was born into a Buckinghamshire family of distinguished ancestry, related by marriage to two significant men of the century, John Hampden and Oliver Cromwell. He inherited a large estate, variously estimated as £2000 to £3500 per year, and lived a long life. He married first an heiress, who died in childbirth, and then a lady about whom little is known except that she bore him thirteen children. Between the two marriages, his courtship of an earl's daughter was fruitless but occasioned his poetic fame. Returned for several constituencies to six or seven parliaments, he was acquainted with four kings (on fairly intimate terms with at least two) and was both a relation and friend of the Lord Protector, Cromwell. The moderate temper of his politics—an idealized constitutional royalism—came into fashion toward the end of his century; he prefigured in this the "peace of the Augustans." In the 1630s he was stimulated by the intellectual company at

15

Great Tew, where Lucius Cary, Viscount Falkland, assembled a
group of remarkable men, including Edward Hyde (later Earl of
Clarendon), George Morley (later Bishop of Winchester), and
Sidney Godolphin. During a period of exile, Waller traveled in
Italy, Switzerland, and France with John Evelyn, and in Paris he
entertained exiled royalists and enjoyed the company of Hobbes,
Gassendi, and Descartes. He lived to see his lyric and compli-
mentary poems become the "official" model for English
Augustan verse. Thomas Rymer wrote for Waller's tomb, in
Latin, a language expected to endure, a judgment upon Waller:
"Of the poets of his day, he was easily the first." In his own day
and in the early eighteenth century, Waller received judicious,
less exaggerated praise from such great writers as John Dryden
and Alexander Pope. As late as 1766 in *Biographia Britannica*
John Campbell asserted that Waller was "the most celebrated
Lyric Poet that ever England produced." But count no man
happy until all his biographers have died. Since 1766, Waller's
reputation has declined; today, his fame for a period of more
than one hundred years is regarded mainly as an oddity in the
history of poetic taste.

Waller's life (1606-1687), sketched in the following pages,
very nearly reached from the death of Queen Elizabeth I to the
Glorious Revolution; his was a century of civil war, political
revolution and evolution, amazing literary achievement; it was
also (as Alfred North Whitehead has written) an age of genius.
Part of Waller's good fortune was to have lived in such an
exciting time.

II *Family and Early Life*

Waller's father Robert married Anne Hampden, sister of the
father of the famous John Hampden. There was, according to
Waller's first biography (published anonymously in the 1711
edition of his poems), a rivalry for honor, power, and property
between the Wallers and the Hampdens. The son of a marriage
of the two families was obliged, or had to feel obliged, to seek
achievement in wealth and public service—and to remember the
family hero Richard Waller, who had fought with distinction
under Henry V. Edmund's father perhaps remembered too well,
for having mainly preoccupied himself with increasing his
wealth, he seemed to have despaired of the quality of his deeds

and, before his death in 1616, prepared for his son a formal admonition to do better.[2]

His mother, a sprightly, resourceful, prudent woman,[3] sent him to school at High Wycombe, near his home, taught by one Mr. Dobson. The pupil followed in his teacher's footsteps, going first to Eton School and then to the university at Cambridge; he was admitted as a fellow-commoner of King's College in 1620. There is no record on his taking a degree.[4]

While still in his teens Waller began a career in the House of Commons which was to last, with some interruptions, for over fifty years. The exact date of his first sitting in Parliament is somewhat uncertain. The inscription on his tomb asserts that he was "not yet eighteen," which is consonant with Clarendon's metaphor that he was "nursed in Parliament, where He sat when He was very young." In debate in the House of Commons, after the Restoration, Waller reminisced that he was sixteen when he first sat in the House.[5] If so, he sat unofficially (and such sitting was customary), for the first record of his being returned is for Ilchester, Somersetshire, in 1624. He was elected to five or six more parliaments during a period of great constitutional struggle.[6]

Waller's early editors and biographers assert that his poetic career, like his political career, was precocious and that the youthful M. P. composed verses immediately after such events as Prince Charles's escape from a storm in 1623 and King Charles's receipt of the news of his favorite Buckingham's death in 1628.[7] But persuasive arguments against such early composition are the absence of any publication of or reference to his poetry until the 1630s, internal evidence suggesting political events of 1635-40, patterns of style connected to datable poems, and the statement of Clarendon that "at the Age when other Men used to give over writing Verses (for He was near thirty Years of Age, when He first engaged himself in that Exercise, at least, that He was known to do so) He surprized the Town with two or three pieces of that Kind; as if a tenth Muse has been newly born, to cherish drooping Poetry."[8]

Although little is recorded of Waller's role in the first parliament of Charles I, the debates of the third in 1628 suggest that Waller was "rapidly coming forward in the House."[9] One is tempted on the basis of bits of information (if he is the Waller whose activities and words are recorded) to see him as somewhat of an enthusiast in religious reform and as part of the progressive, somewhat puritanical alliance of squires and merchants who were later to form the parliamentary side in the Civil Wars and who ultimately triumphed in the Glorious Revolution.

If such was his political stance, it may have been arrested or redirected by his experiences in the 1630s, when (after the parliament of 1628-29 was dismissed) he retired to his county seat in Beaconsfield. Through the mediation of relatives in London, he courted Anne Banks, an heiress whose father had recently died and a ward of the City of London. He married her on July 5, 1631, at St. Margaret's in Westminster, and conveyed her "out the City's jurisdiction into the country." The Court of Aldermen was intent on confiscating her portion of £8000, but the king intervened, pardoned Waller, directed the Aldermen to do the same, and ordered the portion released.[10] Considering the king's great need of revenue at this time, there is a suspicion of some *quid pro quo,* but no helpful records remain. A son was born to the Wallers in 1633, and in the fall of 1634 Anne Waller died after giving birth to a daughter. Unlike the greater models before him, Ben Jonson and John Donne, Waller made no poetic observances of his domestic joys and griefs. Juno, Venus, and sometimes Minerva inspire his poems, but the household gods remain strangers to his muse.

During the interval between parliaments (1629 to 1640), the poetic development described by Clarendon took place; and in this period Waller entered a company of remarkable men at Great Tew who greatly affected his art, his politics, and perhaps his personality. The "Club" which Lucius Cary, Viscount Falkland, founded at Great Tew was made up of a group to which one would *never* have to say, as Cromwell once did to some religious zealots, "I beseech you in the bowels of Christ, think it possible you may be mistaken." It was a Club of bethinkers (George Morley, Roger Chillingworth, Edward Hyde, Sidney Godolphin, Falkland himself), types much to be desired in a society becoming doctrinaire, intolerant, polarized. Nor was elegance any more than sense their aversion, for the Club was devoted to belles lettres, to (for example) Horace as well as Richard Hooker.[11] Idealism, classicism, fairmindedness, moderation, toleration, wit, and ease—these Waller may have, more or less imperfectly, been born with or may have achieved—but his experience in the Club reinforced them all.

Although little is known about his initiation into the Club, Edward Hyde, Earl of Clarendon, has left us important clues about Waller's development and personality. George Morley "assisted, and instructed him in the reading many good Books, to which his natural Parts and Promptitude inclined him, especially the Poets. . . . The Doctor . . . brought him into that Company, which was most celebrated for good Conversation; where He was received, and esteemed, with great Applause, and Respect. He was a very pleasant Discourser, in Earnest, and in Jest, and therefore very grateful to all Kind of Company, where he was not the less esteemed for being very rich."[12]

Probably not before 1636 Waller began to pay court to Dorothy Sidney, the oldest daughter of the Earl of Leicester and the great-niece of Sir Philip Sidney. As the lady in fact (or in the poet's imagination) was haughty and cold, some interest attaches to the name he gave her, Sacharissa, as he said, from "Saccarum, Sugar," presumably because she was sweet. Or perhaps because she was not. Samuel Johnson felt that the name "implies, if it means anything, a spiritless mildness and dull good nature."[13] Apparently the courtship lasted two or three years, until Sacharissa married the Earl of Sunderland, chosen for her by her parents; they at no time considered seriously Waller or any other untitled man and were intent on finding a peer of very high principles. (In Chapter 2, the Sacharissa poems and the question of the degree of seriousness of Waller's poetic courtship will be treated.)

The decade of the 1630s was for Waller a period of development of his natural gifts of courtesy, rhetorical skill, conversation, wit, and poetry. He also improved his economic circumstances by prudent investment in land. And he apparently found time for relationships a bit less exalted than that with Sacharissa. The author of the 1711 *Life* develops rather casually a theme of Waller as the English Petronius; and he comments directly on his love of one kind of pleasure: "It appears by the Verses to *Phillis* and others, Mr. *Waller's* Love for *Sacharissa* did not make him forget what was due to the Beauty of other Ladies, and that they were not all of them so unjust to him, as she whom he of all most admired."[14]

Although some of Waller's poems concern public events that occurred before he was twenty years of age, there is little reason to believe them composed before the 1630s. Clarendon's comments suggest that Waller "surprised the town" with his poems, circulated in manuscripts, in the period of 1635-37. The earliest known publication is a Latin poem on Charles I, printed in an anthology at Cambridge in 1633. Other evidence of his coming to public attention as a poet can be found in his poems themselves: in the title of one poem addressed to the distinguished composer Henry Lawes, we learn that Lawes had "set a song" of Waller's in 1635; and the unequivocal statement of "Phoebus and Daphne" is that the poet achieved poetic fame *during* his courtship of Sacharissa—that is, at some time after the death of Anne Banks Waller (1635) and before the marriage of Dorothy Sidney to the Earl of Sunderland (1639). Other evidence supports the claim of "Phoebus and Daphne": Waller is included in Sir John Suckling's "A Sessions of the Poets," usually dated in the mid-1630s; a poem of Waller's is included in a collection of tributes to Ben Jonson (*Jonsonus Virbius*, 1638); and Sir John Denham pays tribute to Waller in *Coopers Hill*, written in 1639 and published in 1642.

Whatever the problem of dating his political poems, most of the lyric poems—including his best ("Go Lovely Rose!," "On a Girdle," "Stay, Phoebus! Stay," "Of Sylvia," "Peace, Babbling Muse!" and perhaps a dozen more) were almost certainly written during a ten-year period before 1645, the date of their first publication. (These poems are discussed at length in Chapter 2).

The first printed collection of his poems is dated 1645; they were published during the process of his being exiled or after his exile and probably without his authorization. Their publication—with (in several of the 1645 editions or issues) three of his parliamentary speeches—could have been of little advantage to him. The flattering poems to the king and queen could hardly mollify his parliamentary enemies, and the speeches would neither please the royalists nor help their cause. It is however *possible* that the poet or one of his friends had a hand in what appears to be the final version of the collections of 1645 (*Poems, Etc.*/Written By/Mr. Ed. Waller/ . . . Printed for I.N. for Hu. Mosley), which includes the assertion that it was taken from a copy in the poet's own handwriting. Beverly Chew found this edition to be the more nearly perfect of those dated 1645.[15]

III   *For King and Parliament*

Waller may have had little time for poetry from April in 1640, with the opening of the Short Parliament, until the time of his exile at the turn of 1644-45. In the House of Commons during momentous years in British history, he was, a competent, busy, and worthy participant in the most important events. The fairly numerous accounts of his speaking show him to have been an eloquent spokesman for fair play and the opponent of some forms of hypocrisy and inconsistency and a witty teller of home truths; he was, as David Hume noted, as satiric in debate as he was complimentary in verse.[16] In years of growing divisiveness, 1640-43, Waller took a parliamentary position between the two extreme parties, on the model of that of Falkland. A communication of Sir Edward Nicholas to the king, October 29, 1641, concerning a debate in parliament, shows the closeness of the association of Waller, Falkland, and Edward Hyde (later Earl of Clarendon); he wrote that he could "not forbeare" to inform the king that Falkland, Hyde, Waller, and two others had stood as "Champions" in maintaining royal prerogatives and to ask that the king "take some notice . . . for their encouragm't." In the margin, the king wrote: "I co'mande you to doe it in my name, telling them that I will doe it myselfe at my returne."[17] When Falkland agreed to become a counselor to the king (January, 1642), he undoubtedly influenced Waller in a royalist direction.

The records of Waller's participation in debates in the Commons show moderation and independence in the face of increasing hostility. He was in charge of prosecuting Crawley, one of the ship-money judges—those who were impeached by parliament for ruling that the king could require of all counties a levy of money supposedly to finance the building of ships for the navy; this direct form of taxation without consent of parliament had aroused much discontent and protest. Although Waller prosecuted Judge Crawley with some asperity, he also insisted on respecting the rights of Lord Keeper Finch, who was also charged in Parliament with subverting the law in the matter of ship money. Recalling that he was in the Exchequer when the judges voted the legality of ship money and when Finch would not tolerate a general groan, Waller argued for allowing Finch the right to speak in his own defense: it will be praiseworthy, he

said, "if we hear his eloquence that would not hear our groans."
To support his opinion he appealed to the traditions of English
law, as was his custom so often in his long career in the House:
"Though Grand Jury hear not delinquent, yet those that commit
him did. . . . If any of the Grand Jury desire to hear the party
charged, 'tis granted."[18]

Balance, opposition, antithesis, and parallelism are standard
tools of rhetoric and poetry. Their employment—as in Waller's
witty opposition of groans to speech in one's own defense—
usually, perhaps nearly always, communicates a moral point or
general truth. In the case of Finch, the point is that it is wrong
arbitrarily to judge one deemed guilty of *arbitrary* judgment.
This kind of wit, operative in either rhetoric or poetry, often
flourishes when the speaker or the poet confronts extremists.
Perception of such antitheses, parallels, and the like also seems
to derive most genially from a person in the middle, a moderate.
To articulate the perception is to proclaim inconsistency,
hypocrisy, self-deception.

It is also dangerous, as Waller discovered in a set-to with John
Pym, which forms a miniature prototype of Waller's Plot. After
the parliamentary impeachment and execution of the Earl of
Strafford, and during debate on November 6, 1641, Pym
suggested adding to a motion a provision that unless the king
appointed counselors acceptable to Parliament "wee should
account our selves absolved from this ingagement." With
Edward Hyde, Waller opposed the amendment, first reminding
the House that a major charge against the Earl of Strafford was
his advising the king that, unless parliament gave support, the
king was "absolved from" all rules of government: now Pym
advised in a similar way that the House "should pretend that if
the King did not remove his ill Counsellors wee weere absolved
from our duties in assisting him in the Recoverie of Ireland."
Obviously provoked, Pym interrupted Waller on a point of order
and said "that if his motion hee had made weere of the same
nature with the Earle of Straffords then hee deserved the like
punishment." He asked that the House either censure him or
demand an apology of Waller: "Divers called on Mr. Waller to
explaine himselfe which hee not doing fullie, hee was com-
manded after some debate to withdraw, and went accordinglie
into the Committee chamber . . . after a little debate Mr. Waller

was called downe out of the Committee chamber and publikelie asked pardon of the howse and of Mr. Pymme."[19]

The essentially reactive positions of moderates like Waller were controlled by the excesses on the part of the two extreme parties. In January, 1642, the king threatened the leaders of the House—Pym, Hampden, and others—with arrest and impeachment. The City of London rallied to their support as there was widespread concern, certainly shared by Waller, for the liberty and safety of the representatives. Animosity grew as a number from both the Houses went to the king at York, with events leading inevitably to the king's raising his standard at Nottingham on August 25, 1642. When in June of 1642 an attempt at reconciliation was made by Parliament, which had sent a proposal for a peaceful settlement to the king, only to receive an unyielding reply, Waller is reported (often as if to his serious discredit) to have expostulated: "Let us first look to our saifty, and then to our honour."[20] And indeed parliament did exactly so, for the Committee on Public Safety was formed the next month as preparations for war and defense went on apace.

Waller seems to have hesitated when the final break occurred. Clarendon, who of all observers on record probably knew most about his activities, says that he left parliament for a while "when the ruptures grew so great . . . but at the time the standard was set up, having intimacy and friendship with some persons now of nearness about the King [i.e., Hyde himself and Falkland], with the King's approbation, he returned again to London."[21] According to family papers which the writer of the 1711 *Life* claims to have seen, Waller did not leave the House but rather sent *"a Thousand Broad Pieces"* to the King. The Commons Journal, however, records that he had been absent and that the fact of it was a matter of concern on September 2, 1642.[22] In the next few months, November, 1642, to June, 1643, Waller reached a precarious height of political importance, as a man respected in both camps and one of the most visible moderates. Probably the pivotal importance of the middle enabled him to speak freely. Clarendon gives another explanation: "he spoke, upon all occasions, with great sharpness and freedom; which (now there were so few there that used it, and there was no danger of being over-voted) was not restrained; and therefore used as an argument against those, who were gone

upon pretence 'that they were not suffered to declare their
opinion freely in the House; which could not be believed, when
all men knew, what liberty Mr. Waller took, and spoke every day
with impunity, against the sense and proceedings of the
House.' "[23]

IV   Waller's Plot, Arrest, and Escape

Waller's most dashing and disgraceful share in the English civil
wars is the plot to which his name has been attached. The goal of
the plot was to stop the fighting, to bring an end to the opposition
of king and parliament. Of an irenic nature, Waller ventured
more than ever before or afterwards. Over a number of weeks or
months until the end of May, 1643, he engaged in secret
conversations and correspondence with persons in the city, the
parliament, and the court in Oxford (with Hyde and Falkland and
perhaps others); the intention was to bring off a bloodless coup
of the City of London and parliament for the king. It was clear to
him, and certainly true, that the parliament had become
destructive of the traditional order in church and state. His
reading of the forces in the English constitution may have
conditioned the choice he made. The parliament was *now*
uncompromising and *now* unforgiving. The monarch was *now*
uncompromising but *historically* forgiving. The king might do as
he had done before, but who could predict what the parliament
would do? Of course if his plot worked, he would mend the
kingdom and make his fortune over again: "By God!," a fellow
M.P., Symonds D'Ewes, quotes him as saying in glee on the eve of
the plot, "if we can bring to pass this business, we will have
everything!"[24]

    The irony of the plot is that, conceived by moderates (Waller,
Falkland, and Hyde) to influence the middle in a royalist
direction, it had the opposite effect, for Pym used the discovery
of it to intimidate the moderates into a parliamentary commitment. The "vow and covenant" was forced on all the Lords and
Commons after the discovery, a polarization developed between
what was called "the good party" and "the bad," and the point
reached from which there was no going back. Nearly all signed
the covenant: "They who were under the character of moderate
men, and usually advanced all notions of peace and accommodation, durst not oppose the expedient, lest they should be

concluded guilty; most of them having had familiarity with Mr. Waller, and, no doubt, upon sundry occasions, spoken with that freedom to him, as might very well incur a severe interpretation, if upon this occasion, what they had said should be scanned."[25] Further, two of Waller's co-conspirators were quickly tried by court-martial and executed; a number of others were imprisoned. Waller was arrested but not immediately court-martialed because of his privilege as a member of the House of Commons. After a brilliant speech in his own defense, July 4, 1643,[26] he was disenabled from sitting in the House (and therefore subject to prosecution). In his speech he had pleaded that his trial be conducted by the House itself. Kept for a while in close custody, Waller was sent to the Tower of London, where he remained, at least officially, until his release late in 1644.

As John Campbell observed, "His dexterity in saving his life will always be astonishing."[27] Dextrous he was, but not honorable. He gave evidence freely, indeed copiously, against himself and his fellow conspirators; he implicated noble lords and ladies (who were, however, reasonably secure against prosecution); he cooperated fully with Pym, who dramatized the discovery of plot (and deliberately confused it with a military plot led by Sir Nicholas Crispe) in order to terrify the City and Parliament.[28] To his relatives and political friends Waller made craven appeals; these relatives, some rather distant, included the coming man Oliver Cromwell and Sir William Waller, who was one of the two parliamentary generals. He invoked the name of his cousin, the "martyred" John Hampden, with whom he maintained (quite truthfully) he had stood when the king tried to arrest Hampden and four others in January, 1642. In his speech in his own defense in the House, he played upon the members' fear of the army, especially the fear of court-martial. He canted with the zealous preachers on Pym's side, gave them large sums of money, feigned or actually fell into a state of mental distraction, and presented himself as abject and tormented by guilt.[29] All these efforts succeeded, probably because they slowed down efforts to proceed against him, whether in a court-martial or in the House of Commons. The House records show that time and again the question of his trial was postponed.[30] Tempers had time to cool, and greater matters occupied the parliament, especially the need for money to support the army. As early as May, 1644, Waller's friends were at work to make exile his punishment—

even though the zealots in the City of London and in the parliament naturally wanted Waller's head.[31] In September, 1644, Waller petitioned Parliament to remove the sequestration of his estate; this granted, he was able to sell a sizable part of his property, supposedly at a bargain price to a wealthy medical doctor; as John Aubrey puckishly saw it, with £10,000 Waller bribed the whole House. The money was to be used in support of forces newly recruited in the City of London. In September, October, and November a bill gradually made its way through Parliament "that he be put to the Fine of Ten Thousand Pounds" and "banished out of the Realm of *England* and the Dominion of *Wales.*" He was ordered discharged from imprisonment on November 6 and given twenty-eight days to leave.

Waller's behavior during his arrest has incensed many who have taken note of it, none so intensely as some of his contemporaries and Victorian commentators. But his acquaintance and sometime friend, Edward Hyde, has pronounced the judgment that will have to suffice until the last one: Waller preserved his life when he "ought to have been ambitious to have lost it."[32]

V   *Exile, Pardon, and Friendship with Cromwell*

Waller's exile was perhaps more an inconvenience than an ordeal. Before staying for a while in Rouen and Calais in 1645, he married Mary Bresse secretly, either before the plot was discovered or during his long arrest; and (apparently leaving his wife in France) he traveled to Italy in 1646, enrolled for a short time at the University of Padua, and made a leisurely tour with John Evelyn through Italy, Switzerland, and France.[33] Then he settled near Paris and lived elegantly until, pardoned by Parliament November 27, 1651, he returned to England early the next year. A brother-in-law, Colonel Adrian Scroope, is supposed to have interceded with Cromwell on Waller's behalf; the intercession was timely, for, as his first biographer tells, Waller "taking his Lady's Jewels with him to support him . . . was at last come to the *Rump Jewel.*"[34]

Waller wrote few poems during this period, but one relationship developed that was to influence somewhat the values in his verse. During the 1640s and 1650s Waller and Thomas Hobbes became acquainted; it is reported that Hobbes was for a while

tutor to Waller's son. There is evidence in two extant letters that
Waller knew Hobbes's philosophy. In 1645 Hobbes, in Rouen,
wrote to Waller in Calais and thanked him for proposing to
translate *De Cive* into English. Although John Aubrey's anecdotes are not all trustworthy, his explanation of what came of this
project bears all the marks of truth:

I have heard him [Waller] say that he so much admired Mr. Thomas
Hobbes booke *De Cive*, when it came forth, that he was very desirous
to have it donne into English, and Mr. Hobbes was most willing it should
be done by Mr. Waller's hand, for that he was so great a Master of our
English language. Mr. Waller freely promised him to doe it, but first he
would desire Mr. Hobbes to make an Essaye; he (T.H.) did the first
booke, and did it so expremely well, that Mr. Waller would not meddle
with it, for that nobody els could doe it so well.

Aubrey also furnishes information about Waller's dining during
his exile with Hobbes, Gassendi, and Descartes at the table of the
Marquis of Newcastle. In 1657, after Hobbes and Waller had
returned to England, Waller wrote Hobbes a letter that shows
his acquaintance with *The Leviathan* and that makes fairly witty
sport of its detractors. The letter seems written by a disciple, for
it mocks clergymen and praises the autocratic and militaristic
regime of the Protectorate. Aubrey again throws light on the
relationship; he says when he asked Waller to write a eulogy on
Hobbes, Waller refused, stating "that he was afrayd of the
Churchmen: that, what was chiefly to be taken notice of in his
Elogie was that he [Hobbes], being but *one*, and a private
person, pulled-downe all their Churches, dispelled the mists of
Ignorance, and layd-open their Priest-craft." The basis of
Waller's caution—fear—was certainly one Hobbes would have
accepted.[35]

   I suspect that Waller grew to share some of Hobbes's
perceptions about political life. If one describes as "mythic" the
vision of ordered life in Ben Jonson's "To Penshurst," one can say
that Waller's early poems attempt the mythic even as they are
analytical of it. In Jonson, the social life at Penshurst is a unity of
courtesy, generosity, obedience; it is whole, fruitful, pleasant,
pious; hierarchy is natural and pleasant. But the experience of
the 1640s, and I think Hobbes and Waller's reading of it, was that
the mythically sustained hierarchy was destructive of—or could

not preserve—the good, the pleasant things. Religious myth
caused civil war. The aura of kingship could not maintain order.
Waller's political behavior reveals a tension between the
mythical-hierarchical, necessary through custom and nature, and
the good things which the mythic may be analyzed to have
implied: such as the safety of citizens, "law and order,"
ownership of goods, civility, toleration, the social pleasures. I
sense a development in Waller's intellectual life from a Jonsonian
affirmation of mythic tradition, then to a rational, hesitant,
moderate analysis (under the influence of Falkland), and finally
to a skeptical "realism" on the model of Hobbes. During the last
years of his life (see Chapter 4), he became a paragon of
conventional morality and piety. When, operating from the
premises of Hobbes, he uses Jonsonian metaphor and traditional
mythopoeic resources, he produces a peculiarly detached effect
in his poems, which may be either ironic or insincere, but which
seems to have been perceived by the Augustans as sophisticated.

Although Waller was officially pardoned in November, 1651,
arrangements had perhaps been underway earlier in the year,
for in May several members of his family were granted leave to
go to Dover, presumably to visit him and perhaps to accompany
him home. However, for some reason Waller remained in Paris
until January, 1652, possibly to be sure that any dangerous
complications were precluded. His caution was not unjustified, to
judge by the fact that after his return a government order was
sent to Buckinghamshire to direct that he not be harassed.[36]
Having again occasion for laudatory verse, Waller wrote "A
Panegyric to My Lord Protector," which is certainly his best
nonlyric poem.

Clarendon has called attention, hardly in terms of praise, to
Waller's ability to ingratiate himself with those who ordinarily
should have hated or despised him. The ability is that of the
perfectly professional and personally amiable politician; it was so
much Waller's gift that one senses that Charles I, Pym,
Cromwell, Falkland, Hampden, Charles II, and James II all liked
his company.

VI   *Poetry and Politics after the Restoration*

In his life, as in his rhetoric, Waller had the gift of readiness
and quick recovery. He sidestepped execution, lived genteelly in

exile, and returned to England to praise its dictator, Cromwell.
After the Restoration of Charles II, Waller "changed with the
nation" to welcome and praise the king whose father Cromwell
and others had executed. He bestirred himself to attain the role
of royal panegyrist, a role to which he had aspired during the
reign of Charles I. He, John Dryden, and Thomas Sprat each
contributed a poem to make up a book celebrating the
Restoration. Waller's effort—"To the King, Upon His Majesty's
Happy Return" (1660)—was read by the king, who gave directly
to Waller the authoritative opinion that it was inferior to the
panegyric on Cromwell. Waller replied, "We poets succeed
better in fiction than in truth."[37] Perhaps the king encouraged
Waller to better poetic effort, for (besides a number of short
poems celebrating events in the lives of the royal family) Waller
wrote two worthy long poems on Charles and his brother James.
"On St. James's Park" (1661) celebrates the building of a park
enjoyed by the king and people alike; and "Instruction to a
Painter" (1666) celebrates James's naval victory over the Dutch
at Lowestoft.

One must wonder how Waller reinsinuated himself with the
court and the Cavaliers whom he had offended by his escape
from execution and by his praise of Cromwell. Edward Hyde has
left a carefully drawn portrait of Waller which shows how one
old Cavalier felt about him. (Hyde's portrait was probably
written in exile after impeachment proceedings in which Waller
had taken part *against* Hyde.) "There needs no more be said to
extol the Excellence and Power of his Wit, and Pleasantness of
his Conversation, than that it was of Magnitude enough, to cover
a World of very great Faults. . . . [His insinuation and servile
flattery] had Power to reconcile him to those, whom He had
most offended and provoked; and continued to his Age with that
rare Felicity, that his Company was acceptable, where his Spirit
was odious; and He was at least pitied, where He was most
detested."[38] The qualities Clarendon mentions may be viewed
more generously. If amiability enabled Waller to reestablish
himself as a court poet and as a man on the fringe if not in the
midst of matters of public interest, certainly that quality grew
more attractive at a time in which much of the nation wanted to
forgive, or be forgiven, and forget. Closely related to his
amiability was his penchant for reconciliation of conflicting
parties, which was so much strengthened by his years of

experience with extremists that it became a commitment to toleration and moderation, especially in sectarian and politicial issues.

Such is certainly the case in Waller's again becoming a participant in debate in the House of Commons, representing Hastings in the Long Parliament of Charles II (1661-1679). The burning issues were suppression of dissenters and Catholics and the recurrent Stuart problem of revenue for the king and government ("supply"). On the first issue, Waller's numerous recorded speeches, abbreviated in notes taken by Anchitell Grey, are in persistent and witty opposition to the spirit of many, often a majority, of the House who favored various measures of persecution. Waller reminded these zealous Protestants that their forbears were once Catholics; he shrewdly observed that the persecution of sects tended to encourage them and to engender public sympathy: "The people have a kindness for persecuted people, ever since Henry VIII and Queen Mary." In context that could not have pleased, he reminded the House that Christ was kind to the thief "who suffered with him"; therefore, he hoped that "the Papists may be capable of some favour, as well as other Dissenters." On the subject of the different forms of Christianity, he informed his doctrinaire colleagues that Christ is "the sovereign of the Order of the Cross which we all follow."[39]

On the other great issue, taxation or "supply," Waller typically favored (in the recorded debates) giving the king part of what he requested. Although insistent that the role of the Commons was to protect the people against unjust and excessive taxation, he was clearly of the "Country" party, disliking taxation on land and preferring such taxes as import duties, understanding his political preferences as traditional, and wherever possible tending to be deferential to the king. Besides dozens of sharp comments against religious intolerance, as already noted, his comments fall into the following categories: criticism of waste of money by the government and of mismanagement in the navy; insistence on fair play in proceedings against Sir William Penn, Samuel Pepys, and others; habitual assertion of the Commons' rights and privileges when threatened by the House of Lords or the Crown; sometimes tedious recollections of traditional procedures and principles in the parliament. He favored the impeachment of

Clarendon; he spoke in defense of the Duke of York's plans to marry the Catholic Princess of Modena.

Three short extracts from Grey's transcriptions convey the spirit of Waller's speeches in the 1661-79 Parliament: March 17, 1768, in debate on the king's urging toleration, Waller "stands up to prevent the heat that always attends Debates concerning Religion. . . . He repents not his being against severe laws." After pointing out that severe laws have only encouraged the Quakers, he says, "He would not have the Church of *England*, like the elder brother of the Ottoman family, strangle all the younger brothers." March 21, 1676, he joins the debate on supply, having heard "something said, that makes him stand up, for the Honour of King and People. There is no other trust in the Government than where the Law makes it. . . . We believed, when the King was called back, that the Law was come again. . . . Let the King rely upon the Parliament; we have settled the Crown and the Government. 'Tis strange that we have sat so many years, and given so much money, and are still called upon for Supply. . . . Let us look to our Government, Fleet, and Trade. 'Tis the advice that the oldest Parliament-man among you can give you; and so, God bless you!" February 9, 1678, on a point of order whether the Speaker should adjourn the House of Commons immediately as ordered by the king: "In the word immediately the King is extremely concerned, and more than the House, and I see not, without this Question [having a vote on adjournment], how the king can be obeyed. If the Adjournment is immediately to be made upon the King's command, then 'tis to be done *sine medio*. But yet the Message of Adjournment was not sent to the Speaker, but to us, to adjourn ourselves; so that if the Speaker does it, without direction from the House, we cannot obey the King, and I say it for the King's sake. The Schoolmen say, 'God cannot make a thing to be and not to be at the same time.' This freedom of speech [in the House of Commons] could never be taken away."[40]

Contemporary writings, extant manuscripts, and a variety of records give a rosy impression of Waller's life after 1660; a likable and courteous gentleman in the social world, an aging and respected dilletante in the intellectual world, and the elder statesman or viceregent of Apollo in the literary world. He did not, however, please everybody; and before a consideration of his generally comfortable and enviable status, some words might be allowed to his detractors. Clarendon, who knew Waller well for over thirty years, has been quoted earlier on Waller's merits and faults. A younger contemporary historian, Gilbert Burnet, Bishop of Salisbury, knew Waller only in the last decades of his life but drew a portrait somewhat similar in spirit to Clarendon's: "*Waller* was the delight of the House: And even at eighty he said the liveliest things of any among them: He was only concerned to say that which should make him applauded. But he never laid the business of the House to heart, being a vain and empty, tho' a witty, man." The records of debate in the House, discussed above, may show that Burnet described the effect of Waller's style rather than the persistent and substantial concerns of his speeches. Burnet himself said that Waller was one of few "that preserved the Nation from a very deceitful and practising Court, and from a corrupt House of Commons."[41] But clearly, whether in politics or poetry or polite society, Waller's mode of courtesy and panegyric, and perhaps his vanity in them, did not universally please; Lady Ranelagh, writing to her brother Robert Boyle, fixed Waller in formulated phrases: "I know his calling as a poet gives him licence to say as great things as he can, without intending they should signify any more, than that he said them, or have any higher end, than to make him admired by those, whose admirations are so volatile, as to be raised by a sound of words; and the less the subject he speaks of, or the party he speaks to, deserves the great things he says, the greater those things are, and the greater advance they are to make towards his being admired, by his poetical laws."[42]

Like his friend the exiled Frenchman St. Evremond, Waller was a favorite of many ladies, no doubt partly because of the kind of talk that Lady Ranelagh despised. In his correspondence with one of the beauties of the day, Jane Middleton, Waller gave an account of a surprise visit to his Beaconsfield estate: "I have had the honour to receive the Duchess [of York] & Princess [Ann of Denmark] with all their fair train, the Lady Sunderland [Sacharissa's daughter-in-law] was with them who sent me warning but few hours before, and yet they eate heartily & seemed well content with what could so hastily be gotten for them."[43]

His company seems also to have been welcome to Charles II and his brother, as well as to their courtiers. A few anecdotes of his conversations with the two kings survive, mainly ones which show Waller's readiness in conversation.[44] The wits at court may have expected to find in him a Polonius to play to their Hamlet, but were disappointed in this by his facility of conversation. On one occasion Charles and some of his carousing companions made Waller drink so much that he stumbled down the steps of Somerset House and "cracked his skull."[45] After giving up drink, he seems not to have lost their company, according to Samuel Johnson's decorated account: "He passed his time in the company that was highest, both in rank and wit, from which even his obstinate sobriety did not exclude him. Though he drank water he was enabled by his fertility of mind to heighten the mirth of Bacchanalian assemblies; and Mr. [Henry] Saville said, that 'no man in England should keep him company without drinking but Ned Waller.' "[46]

Waller's acquaintance with intellectuals was as wide as that with politicians; and it is likely that through acquaintance at the court, in the Commons, and in the theater he knew nearly everyone of consequence. He was early made a member of the Royal Society, although decidedly more a dilletante than a virtuoso; in later years he was delinquent in paying his dues.[47] If Sir J. Clayton's account of one adventure was typical of Waller's days, he was certainly fortunate: in a letter to Sir Robert Paston, June 8, 1669—"Saturday last I went with the Duke of Buckingham to Denham, with a design to buy it . . . in our return home we dined at Uxbridge, but never in my life did I pass my day away with such gusto, our company being his grace, Mr. Waller, Mr. Surveyor [Christopher] Wren, and myself; nothing but quintessence of wit and most excellent discourse."[48]

In the late seventeenth-century literary world Waller enjoyed an almost incredible position of respect. The playwrights incorporated his poems into their works, most memorably in George Etherege's *Man of Mode* and William Congreve's *The Way of the World.* Poets like Charles Sedley, Rochester, and John Dryden imitated his works and understood themselves as developing further a poetic advance that Waller had initiated. They and others created what René Wellek has called a *fable convenue,* that Waller and John Denham had begun a "refining" of English prosody which was to culminate in the perfected heroic couplet. (This *fable* is treated in Chapter 4.) Dryden also gave authority to the fashion of referring to Waller as "Mr.

Waller," which curiously continued in the eighteenth century and has been used more recently, to ironic and unsympathetic purpose, by F. R. Leavis. Dryden has taken care that his assessment of Waller be unambiguous; referring to him as "the father of our English numbers," he wrote, "I hope the reader need not be told, that Mr. Waller is only mentioned for honour's sake; that I am desirous of laying hold on his memory of all occasions, and thereby acknowledging to the world, that unless he had written, none of us could write."[49] (This remarkable praise is discussed in Chapter 4.)

Solid evidence of Waller's popularity as a poet (and inferential evidence of his influence on others) is to be found in the publishing history of his poems. In 1660 the 1645 issues of his collected poems were in demand but scarce and expensive. After a new edition in 1664, his publisher Henry Herringman appears to have kept the poems in print, for there appeared new editions with additional poems in 1668, 1682, and 1686. To judge by the frequency with which these are encountered today in the antiquarian book trade and by the number of copies held by libraries, Herringman's printings were rather large. Waller also published individual poems such as "Instructions to a Painter" (1666), which occasioned a number of replies or parodies, and the collection *Divine Poems* (1685); *Pompey the Great*, published in 1664, was translated from Corneille's *Mort de Pompée* by Waller, Charles Sackville, Charles Sedley, and others. Additional poems and his revision of *The Maid's Tragedy* appeared posthumously in 1690, with a preface usually attributed to Francis Atterbury.

The poems published after the Restoration do not justify the opinion of his early critics that he wrote uniformly well throughout his life. The three important political poems—"To the King, Upon His Majesty's Happy Return" (1660), "On St. James's Park" (1661), and "Instructions to a Painter" (1666)—are not of the brilliance of the panegyric to Cromwell, although more unified and more carefully crafted than those written to Charles I. Rarely, a lyric—like "Chloris, Farewell"—or an occasional poem—like "To a Fair Lady, Playing with a Snake"—seem worthy of comparison to a score or so jewel-like poems published in 1645. "Of English Verse" and "Upon Roscommon's Horace" are worthy poems; but his last major effort, *The Divine Poems* (1685), proves not so much Johnson's view that it is impossible to write poetry about religious devotion or "contemplative piety" as that it was not possible for Waller in his late seventies to write such poetry well.

Waller died October 21, 1687, and was buried in Beaconsfield churchyard. "By a curious piece of irony," as Waller's editor G. Thorn-Drury has pointed out, Waller was buried dressed in wool, in accordance with an act of Parliament designed to protect a national industry. Waller had opposed this very act when it was debated in the House of Commons, in his usual manner appealing to tradition and finding a sharp allusion which must have pained even as it failed to persuade his adversaries: "Our Savior was buried in linen. 'Tis a thing [being buried in woolen] against the Customs of Nations, and I am against it."[50]

In 1688 appeared *Poems to the Memory of That Incomparable Poet Edmond Waller.* In it, St. Evremond, his French friend and counterpart in courtesy, accounted for the longevity of Waller, who "S'attache â la Beauté pour vivre plus long temps." In agreement with several other contributors who praised Waller's "refinement" of English verse and his achievement in love poetry, Aphra Behn asserted that he taught poets "how to Love, and how to Write." Thomas Rymer, who also wrote the epitaph for a monument erected in Beaconsfield in 1700, emphasized Waller's parliamentary career (perhaps because he reserved for *A Short View of Tragedy,* 1693, his praise of Waller's poems): "What Life, what Lightning blanch'd around the *Chair?*/(It was no *House,* if *Waller* was not there:)/. . . . Thus [against intolerance] would he play, and many a pointed Jest/Still fling against the persecuting Beast."

Although exaggerated, these comments and the other eulogies in *Poems to the Memory of . . . Waller* embody important truths. Waller's life was a long and happy one; he enjoyed a natural felicity of personality and artistry; he had a gift for drawing the good and the beautiful from persons and things. His career in Parliament was, on the whole, worthy and elegant. His poems, widely admired themselves, were also thought to have made possible the achievements of the great Augustan poets.

CHAPTER 2

Songs and Lyrical Epigrams

I *The Types of Waller's Writings*

BECAUSE Waller is a poet without a strong sense of genre, his one hundred fifty-odd poems do not divide easily into clear and distinct categories. Most are occasional poems, or "epigrams" (in the broad sense of Jonson's *Epigrams*), which are nearly always about love, politics, or art. A smaller group is similarly occasional, but follows more the tradition of the epistle (as found in Horace, Donne, Jonson, Carew, Herrick, Lovelace) and usually concerns the same topics. The most memorable are the songs, about twenty in number, identified as such by the designation in the text (by the poet or the printer) or by their being set to music by Henry Lawes.[1] Another twenty, less important, fall into the following types: epitaph, epigram (in the strict sense of a short poem with a pointed, often satiric conclusion), mock epic, translation, prologue, epilogue, pastoral elegy.

Since most of Waller's poems are poems of praise, the term panegyric is useful[2] but should be reserved to describe the long, formal poems. These are generally political—e.g., addressed to a king or concerned with the navy or a war—and can well be named "panegyrical epigrams" or panegyrical epistles (*pace* Polonius), thus specifying the genre and purpose (although the purpose is rarely *merely* to praise). In these, as in the "epigrams" or occasional poems about art or love, Waller uses the occasion to discover and to make discriminations in the worthiness (the human values) of events and relationships. As the "epigrams" about love, courtship, struggle, and conciliation of the sexes resemble in content and form the songs proper, they may be described as "lyrical epigrams."

Waller contributed to two significant subgenres of the occasional: (a) the painter poem—"Instructions to a Painter" and (b) the loco-descriptive (or topographical)—"On St. James's Park." (An earlier poem had influenced John Denham's *Coopers Hill*, the most famous seventeenth-century poem of this type.)[3] Waller's literary and rhetorical productions also include some few extant letters, completion of his friend Sidney Godolphin's translation of the fourth book of *The Aeneid*, a translation of one act of Corneille's *Mort de Pompée*, an alteration of John Fletcher's *Maid's Tragedy*, and parliamentary speeches (four printed *in toto* and many summarized in various records of debates in the House of Commons).

I propose to discuss the poems in three groups: songs and lyrical epigrams—using the term "epigram" to signify a poem exploring the meaning of an event or a relationship (Chapter 2); panegyrical epigrams and epistles concerning political figures and events (Chapter 3); and epigrams and epistles concerning art and artists (Chapter 4).

II   *Patterns in the Lyrics*

Much of the pleasure and wit of seventeenth-century poetry derives from the shared culture of the poet and his audience. Waller's reply to Charles II, who pointed out the superiority of his verse on Cromwell, illustrates the typical awareness of poet and public: "we poets succeed better in fiction than in truth." The appeal is to the widespread principle of Renaissance criticism that poets "deliver a golden" world and to the difficulty, faced by poet and courtier alike, of finding compliments adequate to the golden expectations of French and English royalty. The reply is an escape from the difficulty and wittily hides the brazen truth in a present fiction. The point derives from the knowing—by the king, and Waller, and the public audience—of the tradition of poetic idealization and the rigors of courtesy.

It is the ironic play generated by the shared culture, the participants and speakers, and the audience that renders subtle and fascinating the Wallerian poem at its best—with the concession, of course, that the excellence is not grand or ultimate. The critics have almost with one eye perceived Waller to be a poet "limited in scope," or the "leader of a restrictive moment," or (in the most recent full-scale study) "the poet of limitation." I wish in this chapter to analyze first a number of songs and lyrical epigrams which illustrate his rhetorical deftness and imaginative facility and then to consider several poems on Cavalier themes.

Critics agree that Waller's skill is in "the witty use of myth," or in "raising modern Compliments upon ancient Story, and setting off the British Valour and the English Beauty, with the old Gods and Goddesses."[4] The pagan deities were an irresistible poetic resource, as witness Thomas Carew's "Elegy upon the Death of Doctor Donne." A major argument in praise of John Donne is that he rid his poems of references to the ancient gods and goddesses and freed poets from servile imitation of the classics. Previous to him, English poets had performed "Licentious thefts, that make poetic rage/ A mimic fury." Now, Carew fears, Donne's death means a return to constricting neoclassicism.

> But thou art gone, and thy strict laws will be
> Too hard for libertines in poetry.
> They will repeal the goodly exil'd train
> Of gods and goddesses, which in thy just reign
> Were banish'd nobler poems; now, with these,
> The silenc'd tales o' th' *Metamorphoses*
> Shall stuff their lines, and swell the windy page.

Yet this very poem, a protest against such "stuffing," includes nonironic allusion to the Delphic oracle, to Prometheus, and to the Muses. And it builds to a conclusion with an elaborate metaphor on a "crown of bays" and ends with the following turn: "Here lie two flamen, and both these the best:/ Apollo's first, and last the true God's priest."[5] In England in the 1630s one encountered the myths in every place of daily life—walls, ceilings, gardens, the accouterments of the household—as well as in masques, epics, and songs.

Waller's habit is to discover in an occasion an honorific parallel to the myths: precisely the opposite of the mock-epic. His strategy in the use of mythic "applications"—I borrow the term from "The Story of Phoebus and Daphne, *Applied*"[6]—is to *find* the analogy in the context of the event. In the poem on Prince

Charles's escape from a storm in 1623 (written later), Waller imagines Charles fearless in a small boat at sea thinking of his future bride Henrietta: "he had seen a brighter nymph than she/ That sprung out of his present foe, the sea" (ll. 103-04). The "easiness" of the application depends on its flowing from the scene (springing from the sea and action) and on the strong possibility that the audience will *anticipate* the association. Even in the next few lines, where the poet mentions Thetis by name, he does so in reference to the scene already painted: "That noble ardor, more than mortal fire,/ The conquered ocean could not make expire;/ Nor angry Thetis raise her waves above/ The heroic Prince's courage or his love" (ll. 105-08). Too rich to be easy, however, is the presence, in this one poem of 170 lines, of the many allusions to Bacchus, Jove, Orion, Mars, Neptune, Phaeton, Aeneas, Priam, Thetis, Aurora, Cupid, Jason, Theseus, Leander, Musaeus, Hero, the Fates, and Ovid.

The songs and lyrical "epigrams" are perhaps more secure against oblivion than the political and panegyrical verse because of a more sparing and hence more artful use of application. This device, in the much-admired "The Story of Phoebus and Daphne, Applied," is central to the skill in management of tone and irony:

> Thyrsis, a youth of the inspired train,
> Fair Sacharissa loved, but loved in vain.
> Like Phoebus sung the no less amorous boy;
> Like Daphne she, as lovely, and as coy!
> With numbers he the flying nymph pursues,
> With numbers such as Phoebus' self might use!
> Such is the chase when Love and Fancy leads,
> O'er craggy mountains, and through flowery meads;
> Invoked to testify the lover's care,
> Or form some image of his cruel fair.
> Urged with his fury, like a wounded deer,
> O'er these he fled; and now approaching near,
> Had reached the nymph with his harmonious lay,
> Whom all his charms could not incline to stay.
> Yet what he sung in his immortal strain,
> Though unsuccessful, was not sung in vain;
> All, but the nymph that should redress his wrong,
> Attend his passion, and approve his song.
> Like Phoebus thus, acquiring unsought praise,
> He catched at love, and filled his arm with bays.[7]

In contrast to most of the other Sacharissa poems, the speaker is assertive, although perhaps his shadow hangs back. The "real" circumstance is that he has become famous and the girl exists now only as a wreath. The poet, courteous in an undercutting counterpoint, alludes to her error: "All, but the nymph that should redress his wrong/ Attend his passion, and approve his song." In images with two tenors (the struggle of art and the ordeal of the lover) he makes his case against her: "Such is the chase when Love and Fancy leads,/ O'er craggy mountains, and through flowery meads;/ Invoked to testify the lover's care/ Or form some image of his cruel fair." The assertive comparison of the poet to Apollo is not without peril to the tone, as in the line "Yet what he sung in his immortal strain," which is almost silly unless *strain* is a pun. The same is true of "Like Phoebus sung the no less amorous boy," in which the modesty of Waller the *boy* (whether it means "the youth" or the traditional "swain" of love poetry) balances the arrogance of success implied in the comparison to Apollo.

Warren Chernaik has said that the "theme is the relationship between life and art."[8] Or, more narrowly stated, the working by art of good out of suffering. But the poem is also about the poet's feeling as a man, rejected yet self-assured and self-assuring, with the witty addendum that the lady *proved* herself wrong. The application, the poet as Apollo, is worked into a complex comment on a delicate situation.

Possibly in the application Waller realized his peculiar excellences, an easiness in blending the colors of rhetoric with those of his subject and unclichéd reference to well-known and immediately recollected literature and art. In the application is found the accent of his poetic voice which distinguishes him from Jonson and the Cavaliers. Jonson, knowing how hard-bought learning is, preserves the distinction between the esoteric and the exoteric in his references; Richard Lovelace tends toward the almost private allegory; Robert Herrick is more interested in shared ritual; Andrew Marvell prefers the mystically emblematic; and John Suckling unallusive eccentricity.

Increasingly, since the time of the Victorian critics (or post-Wordsworthians) the perception of readers is that there is no "true" feeling in the Sacharissa poems. In such a perception the biographical issues and the reading of the poems mutually obfuscate each other; the reader predecides that, there being no romance, the poems are unimpassioned; or that, the poems being unimpassioned, the romance was nonexistent. Consider Thorn-Drury's response: "Aubrey says that he [Waller] was passionately in love with the lady, and even goes so far as to suggest that his rejection by her was probably the cause of a fit of madness. . . . Nothing in the verses which Waller addressed to Sacharissa has been more remarked than the absence of anything like the appearance of passion."[9] It is no longer necessary to defend a poet's speaking in a public voice, or to demonstrate that rhetorical contrivance is not inauthentic legerdemain.

The Sacharissa poems (the sixteen poems—one repeated in Latin—printed in Thorn-Drury's edition, I, 43–65) seem to me in earnest. Contrived to win a lady high-born and disdainful, the persuasiveness of the poems is undercut by the speaker's awareness that he is failing, and perhaps the tentativeness is part of the rhetoric. There is in any good Waller poem (in any good Cavalier poem) play of awareness, often an awareness of the limit of the present enthusiasm. The poet in this case knows he is overreaching and doomed; thus he is at once ingenious in his assertion and tentative, self-protective. "To Vandyck" illustrates a complex of such vectors: The painter is a "Rare Artisan, whose pencil moves/ Not our delights alone, but loves!"—a power the poet would like to share, the poet who yet counsels himself well: "Fool! that forgets her stubborn look/ This softness from thy [Vandyck's] finger took."[10] Clarity about passion is not "absence" of passion, at least not to Waller and the Cavalier poets. Thorn-Drury misses the intensity in analyses of passion, often the essential virtue or excellence in seventeenth-century poems. A good example of this worth, of the interplay of feeling and awareness, is Suckling's "dispassionate" advice to Carew in "Upon my Lady Carlisle's Walking in Hampton Court Garden." The speaker (Suckling) tried to persuade the enthusiastic admirer (Carew) that the lady's beauty is a subjective creation of the admirer. The advice is intense *and* detached. "I must confess those perfumes (Tom)/I did not smell; nor found that from/ Her passing by, ought sprung up new,/ The flowers had all their birth from you." The Cavalier response to Thorn-Drury is, I believe, that one does not have to be simple or foolish to be passionate.

In nearly half the Sacharissa poems, the themes concern the relationship of art (poetry) to love: the awareness of a wider audience, the poetic victory in defeat, the poet's better claim to

Sir Philip Sidney as ancestor, the inferiority of art to natural
beauty except for the mortality of the latter. The brief cycle of
poems presents Waller's discovery of his role as an artist and of
the consoling and transcending values of poetry. The Sacharissa
episode, insofar as it has been recorded, had an appropriately
graceful conclusion. When Dorothy married Lord Sunderland,
Waller wrote to Lucy, her younger sister, a gallant letter which
includes this paragraph:

May she [Sacharissa] that always affected Silence and Retiredness,
have the House fill'd with the Noise and Number of her Children, and
hereafter of her Grand-Children, and then may she arrive at that great
Curse so much declin'd by fair Ladies, Old Age: May she live to be very
old, and yet seem young, be told so by her Glass, and have no Aches to
inform her of the Truth: And when she shall appear to be mortal, may
her Lord not mourn for her, but go Hand in Hand with her to that
Place, where we are told there is neither marrying nor giving in
Marriage, that being there divorced, we may all have an equal Interest
in her again. My Revenge being immortal, I wish all this may also befall
their poste[rity] to the Worlds End, and Afterwards.[11]

A man may be teasing, gallant, and witty—and quite moved.

In many poems, Waller's scope is through the lens of the epic
to the contemporary. Dryden and Pope, who followed Waller
and others in such a poetic method, have in their greater
achievements accustomed us to such a scope and to the
discoveries it makes, that some human actions are noble (epic-
like) and some pitiful, absurd, evil (unheroic or heroic in the
wrong direction). Waller's legacy to these greater poets is the
skill in making the perception seem natural and the judgments it
implies inevitable. "The Fall" furnishes an excellent example,
wherein the applications are especially unobtrusive.

The Fall

> See! how the willing earth gave way,
> To take the impression where she lay.
> See! how the mould, as loth to leave
> So sweet a burden, still doth cleave
> Close to the nymph's stained garment. Here
> The coming spring would first appear,
> And all this place with roses strow,
> If busy feet would let them grow.

Here Venus smiled to see blind chance
Itself before her son advance,
And a fair image to present,
Of what the boy so long had meant.
'Twas such a chance as this, made all
The world into this order fall;
Thus the first lovers on the clay,
Of which they were composed, lay;
So in their prime, with equal grace,
Met the first patterns of our race.
Then blush not, fair! or on him frown,
Or wonder how you both came down;
But touch him, and he'll tremble straight,
How could he then support your weight?
How could the youth, alas! but bend,
When his whole heaven upon him leaned?
If aught by him amiss were done,
'Twas that he let you rise so soon.

I am tempted to call this "heroic-lyric." An ordinary event in a courtship acquires, gracefully, cosmic proportions, even as the poem excels as an exposition of a relationship. Details are seen through the epic perceptivity of the poet. The earth courteously gave way when the lady lay upon it, a suggestive enough beginning for a love poem. It adoringly clung when she rose, clung to a garment now stained; the lady's touch has made the place fecund, if its innocence, ironically, could be maintained against the "busy feet" of the world. The accident of the fall pleases Venus, for it is the platonic idea of Cupid's caprice. "What the boy so long had meant" is grandly imagined; Cupid had yet to achieve such a *falling* in love. This fall is an emblem of the first Fall, which becomes (as the poet shifts to the Lucretian theory of creation to exhaust the *pre-collections* of this event) the "chance that made all/ The world into this order fall."

The argument is that the lady should not resent that she fell, nor the man either, seeing the epic meanings that her fall recaptured or sponsored. Of course, the fall acquires more explicitly a sense of sexual transgression at this point, and the concern of the poet is to reveal the heroic weight that brought the man down (and thus to excuse him). "How could the youth, alas! but bend,/ When his whole heaven upon him leaned?" The gallant or bawdy reversal at the end preserves the earlier overtones of erotic fecundity and the paradox of the *felix culpa*. If the fall was good, it was then wrong to end it so soon. If an actual seduction is delicately represented as a fall in the path, the couplet is ironic in more naturalistic terms.

The reader can, with little fear of disappointment, expect clarity in Waller's images and applications. Yet, since Waller relies on common recollection of the cultural inheritance, he can create a certain effect by subduing his penchant for the perspicacious and letting the "perfect" or clichéd mythic parallel force itself through the writer's page to the reader's attention.

On a Girdle

That which her slender waist confined,
Shall now my joyful temples bind;
No manarch but would give his crown,
His arms might do what this has done.

It was my heaven's extremest sphere,
The pale which held that lovely deer.
My joy, my grief, my hope, my love,
Did all within this circle move!

A narrow compass! and yet there
Dwelt all that's good, and all that's fair;
Give me but what this ribband bound,
Take all the rest the sun goes round.

This poem has been praised for its treatment of an ancient theme, the "preoccupation with some intimate object associated with one's mistress," and sharply analyzed into "a succession of circles, variations upon the theme of surrounding, enclosing, encircling, encompassing."[12] But the repressed application is of the girdle of Venus, famous for its erogenous powers, which makes man and god forget everything except love and desire. The speaker reacts as hyperbolically as Jove when Juno inveigled him with Venus's magic girdle: bewitched by magical beauty, he is induced to see everything outside the female as valueless. And the images of encirclement and confinement make the point emphatic. If the allusion is to the night of love which kept Jove away from the Trojan War, there is reinforcement to the suggestion in the first two lines that the speaker's euphoria ("joyful temples") derives from some proof of the lady's love.

The poem also illustrates a second standard Wallerian rhetorical device, the turn, wherein the poet repeats a word or idea, as in the idea of encirclement which is repeated, in a series of arabesques, in nearly every line. The turn derives from a musical pattern in which one note is played twice, first with a higher, then with a lower accompanying note. George Puttenham's elaborate analysis of rhetorical figures includes a variety of forms of the turn. The simplest perhaps is "a figure which the Latines call *Traductio,* and I the tranlacer: which is when ye turne and tranlace a word into many sundry shapes as the Tailor doth his garment, & after that sort do play with him in your dittie." A more complex turn, the *antimetabole* uses two words: "Ye have a figure which takes a couple of words to play with in a verse, and by making them to chaunge and shift one into others place they do very pretily exchange and shift the sence."[13] The device was much less pleasing to Samuel Butler, who denounced Waller's use of it as "teasing with sense" and predicted it would grow out of fashion![14] The effects sought in the turn are emphasis, poignancy, and irony, as in the related devices antithesis and parodox. For example, consider these lines from "Of a Lady Who Can Sleep When She Pleases": "Wise Somnus to that paradise repairs;/ Waits on her will, and *wretches* does forsake,/ To court the nymph for whom those *wretches* wake" (italics mine). The rhyme (verbs associated with the repeated noun) and the alliteration reinforce the point. Frequently the turn is strengthened by other colors of rhetoric such as elaborate balance of meter and sound, oxymoron, chiasmus: "In love the victors from the vanquished fly:/ They fly that wound, and they pursue that die."

Resembling the circular turns in "On a Girdle" is the play on ideas of size ("little," "frame," "measure out," "humble," "beneath," "over," "high," "mountains," Polypheme) in the delightful poem "Of the Marriage of the Dwarfs."

> Design, or chance, makes others wive:
> But Nature did this match contrive;
> Eve might as well have Adam fled,
> As she denied her little bed
> To him, for whom Heaven seemed to frame,

And measure out, this only dame.
  Thrice happy is that humble pair,
Beneath the level of all care!
Over whose heads those arrows fly
Of sad distrust and jealousy;
Secured in as high extreme,
As if the world held none but them.
  To him the fairest nymphs do show
Like moving mountains, topped with snow;
And every man a Polypheme
Does to his Galatea seem;
None may presume her faith to prove;
He proffers death that proffers love.
  Ah, Chloris, that kind Nature thus
From all the world had severed us;
Creating for ourselves us two,
As love has me for only you!

Discovering the epic dimensions in the love of dwarfs, Waller develops the antitheses in an urbane, amused tone to reveal their good fortune. They are made for each other, a little Adam and Eve; they are *raised* to the happiness of being *beneath* jealousy. Almost half the lines of the poem emphasize some paradox of the large values of their smallness. Their ultimate worth is that the poet himself envies them, wishing for the same fated love with Chloris, whom he addresses. And the poet's capacity to see the luck of the dwarfs is revealed in the fact that he himself is dwarfed by love—"As love has me for only you." The plaintive note is that Chloris is not so dwarfed and the two of them not thus sequestered from the world.

A common statement in biographies of Waller is that he wrote as well at eighty as at thirty. Whereas he does hit off some fine lines in his very last poems and in two or three short poems published after 1660—I exclude here judgment of the longer, political poems—there is not to be found the wholeness and inevitability of design typical of a number of small poems first published in 1645. For example, "To a Fair Lady, Playing with a Snake" has all the ingredients of the earlier gems (turn, application, zeugma, oxymoron, antithesis) and builds to a fairly pointed conclusion. But it lacks coherence and focus.

Strange! that such horror and such grace
Should dwell together in one place;
A fury's arm, an angel's face!

'Tis innocence, and youth, which makes
In Chloris' fancy such mistakes,
To start at love, and play with snakes.

By this and by her coldness barred,
Her servants have a task too hard;
The tyrant has a double guard!

Thrice happy snake! that in her sleeve
May boldly creep; we dare not give
Our thoughts so unconfined a leave.

Contented in that nest of snow
He lies, as he his bliss did know,
And to the wood no more would go.

Take heed, fair Eve! you do not make
Another tempter of this snake;
A marble one so warmed would speak.

Why is the snake "thrice happy"—especially in view of poetic overtones in the phrase? He plays with her, he guards her, he can creep in her sleeve? He has the lady, he has no rivals, he achieves what others imagine? What does the repetitious fifth stanza add? If only the antithesis of cold to the warming of stanza six, why no more witty connection? The elements of the poem, while fascinating, remain desultory. The rhetorical devices keep vividly before us the lady's misconceptions about love and temptation, much the same as Belinda's in Alexander Pope's *The Rape of the Lock:* if she behaves so provocatively, she may be tempted in a more blunt manner. And if the lady's body is imagined as a paradise, then the snake's presence (at her instance) is anomalous, dangerous, and represents a home truth: the lady should warm up or stop tempting. Interestingly, too, Waller goes to oblique communication via allusion (to Eve) as he approaches the physical realities of love, thus keeping genteel and delicate circumstances of what the Wife of Bath calls "oure bothe thinges smalle."

The error of allowing Waller very little imaginative power is avoided by the reader who recalls that a person in a quiet voice may say the wittiest things and that often the quietness enhances the wit, as in the song "Stay, Phoebus! Stay.":

> Stay, Phoebus! stay;
> The world to which you fly so fast,
> Conveying day
> From us to them, can pay your haste
> With no such object, nor salute your rise,
> With no such wonder as De Mornay's eyes.
>
> Well does this prove
> The error of those antique books,
> Which made you move
> About the world; her charming looks
> Would fix your beams, and make it ever day,
> Did not the rolling earth snatch her away.

The movement of Waller's "reform" in verse was to place wit in smooth settings rather than in rough clusters. Or, if wit is a jewel-like decoration in art, the concern is to blend the other elements with the decoration so as to render an effect of unlabored harmony of idea, image, sound, rhyme. That this is unlike Donne's procedure has been often remarked.[15] In "Stay, Phoebus! Stay" the wit falls into two parts. In one, the poet assumes the Ptolemaic universe and compliments the lady by wondering why the sun should leave her in his circuit through the sky. In the second, the older theory is rejected, and the lady's noneffect on the sun is demonstrative proof (a most satisfactory virtuoso demonstration or experiment) that the sun does not move, for the only explanation is that the earth moves her from him.

A sly and cunning art works by implication behind striking utterance, as in "Behold the Brand of Beauty Tossed":

> Behold the brand of beauty tossed!
> See how the motion does dilate the flame!
> Delighted love his spoils does boast,
> And triumph in this game.
> Fire, to no place confined,
> Is both our wonder and our fear;
> Moving the mind,

As lightning hurled through the air.
High heaven the glory does increase
Of all her shining lamps, this artful way;
The sun in figures, such as these,
Joys with the moon to play;
To the sweet strains they advance,
Which do result from their own spheres,
As this nymph's dance
Moves with the numbers which she hears.

The theme is the interaction of woman's beauty and beauty in the arts of dance, music, and poetry. The motion of the dance enhances the woman's beauty, as the striking beginning affirms. The worthiness of this is confirmed by the analogy of the sun and the moon in gracefully related motion to the music of the spheres. As this song itself presumably is danced by the nymph, she moves to the poet's numbers, suggesting a relationship of mutual love and motion on the pattern of sun and moon. Although the attributing of brightness to (or the discovery of it in) the beautiful is at least as old as Homer and the Old Testament, and although Waller makes a habit of using images of light in praise of ladies, he here elevates the habitual into imaginative forms as striking as the beauty he describes. The brightness of the verse moves, too.

Waller expiates his fond overuse of the cliché *bright-beauty* in a later poem entitled "The Night-piece" where the challenge to wit is to find reasons (of course non-bawdy) for praise of a lady when she is in the dark. There, unblinded by her face, he can appreciate the sound of her voice, her mind (imaged in stars otherwise hidden by her beauty, the sun), her breath:

All near approaches threaten death;
We may be shipwrecked by her breath;
Love, favoured once with that sweet gale,
Doubles his haste, and fills his sail,
Till he arrive where she must prove
The haven, or the rock, of love.
So we the Arabian coast do know
At distance, when the spices blow;
By the rich odour taught to steer,
Though neither day nor stars appear[.]

The discovery of unsuspected powers and virtues, or the good in the apparently bad, is Waller's poetic goal. Perhaps happiness as well as anxiety is an authentic human mode, whether instinctive-biological or achieved by struggle, as in "À La Malade."

> Ah, lovely Amoret! the care
> Of all that know what's good or fair!
> Is heaven become our rival too?
> Had the rich gifts, conferred on you
> So amply thence, the common end
> Of giving lovers—to pretend?
>   Hence, to this pining sickness (meant
> To weary thee to a consent
> Of leaving us) no power is given
> Thy beauties to impair; for heaven
> Solicits thee with such a care,
> As roses from their stalks we tear,
> When we would still preserve them new
> And fresh, as on the bush they grew.
>   With such a grace you entertain,
> And look with such contempt on pain,
> That languishing you conquer more,
> And wound us deeper than before.
> So lightnings which in storms appear,
> Scorch more than when the skies are clear.
>   And as pale sickness does invade
> Your frailer part, the breaches made
> In that fair lodging, still more clear
> Make the bright guest, your soul, appear.
> So nymphs o'er pathless mountains borne,
> Their light robes by the brambles torn
> From their fair limbs, exposing new
> And unknown beauties to the view
> Of following gods, increase their flame,
> And haste to catch the flying game.

This is probably Waller's most bizarre theme, that the sickness of Amoret is the courtship of the gods. Out of the opening assertion that Amoret is the care of "all that know what's good and fair"— presumably including the gods—the gods' interest in her is discovered by the poet, their rival. With the next discovery, that her beauty is unimpaired by their interest, comes the analogy to cut roses (which is not too persuasive, as the roses will fade). But the unintended result of the gods' rivalry is that the rival is all the more smitten by the lady's stoicism, for the ills of the body reveal the goods of the soul. "And as pale sickness does invade/ Your frailer part, the breaches made/ In that fair lodging, still more clear/ Make the bright guest, your soul, appear." Since Waller was to use that image again in a serious poem, "Of the Last Verses in the Book," I assume it had a special meaning for him and, in view of the consolation offered for illness, conclude that the lady too must have been affected. The charm here as elsewhere is that a common event (a lady's illness) with common feelings (her depression, the concern of her friends, the wish to cheer her up) is reworked by the poet to maximize the pleasant. This is not to flatter but to realize the happy moments in human life. Much of the limitation in Waller is due to his cultivation of the normal, the healthy-minded, as can best be seen in his poetic "debate" with Sir John Suckling.

"In Answer of Sir John Suckling's Verse" (first printed in 1645) was made by Waller's mating lines of counterargument with sections of Suckling's "Against Fruition." The result is not only a battle of wit (or a mock-battle controlled by Waller) but also a contest of sensibilities. In his poem Suckling elaborates a traditional sexual experience (idealized expectancy becoming disappointing reality) into an erotic system presented by a roué to a "fond youth" apparently engaged in a seduction: *"ask no more; be wise;/ Knowing too much, long since lost Paradise."* The analogies Suckling finds to support his case generate appeals to a subjective, decadent aestheticism: better to dream of sex than let crude reality bore you. (Or, as Samuel Beckett has it, the pornographer alone on a desert island is *the* happy man.) Waller reverses—*turns* on—Suckling's analogies, as in his reply to the couplet just quoted: "And, by your knowledge, we should be bereft/ Of all that paradise which yet is left." Or consider the last exchange in the poem:

Con. [Suckling]
They, who know all the wealth they have, are poor;
He's only rich that cannot tell his store.

Pro. [Waller]
Not he that knows the wealth he has is poor,
But he that dares not touch, nor use, his store.

Waller expresses in an uncommon way the attitudes and passions of the average man—*l'homme moyen sensuel.* He is vitally

normal, an extraordinary spokesman for the ordinary good things
(consider the extreme way he insisted on the goodness of life in
escaping execution). In this respect, he is much like Thomas
Hobbes, who goes for his proofs to ordinary experience, urging
men and women to look into themselves for the evidence.[16]

III   *Cavalier Themes and Insights*

Several of Waller's best poems, and his most famous poem,
develop the *carpe diem* theme. Perhaps they are better styled
"invitations to enjoy," for *seizing* the day has too strong a note of
action to describe poems made to possess some of the fragility or
softness of the ladies they address. The formula for a Wallerian
invitation is to persuade slyly by telling the lady what she likes to
hear; artfully contrived, polished, melodious, the poem must
seem to be simple, sincere, artless. Many of the poems have
Latin, French, or English models but work in ingenious and novel
ways to find the value of love, even in what often seems to be the
unfortunate concomitants of love.[17] "To Phyllis" furnishes a good
example of the pattern:

> Phyllis! why should we delay
> Pleasures shorter than the day[?]
> Could we (which we never can[)]
> Stretch our lives beyond their span,
> Beauty like a shadow flies,
> And our youth before us dies.
> Or would youth and beauty stay,
> Love hath wings, and will away.
> Love hath swifter wings than Time;
> Change in love to heaven does climb.
> Gods, that never change their state,
> Vary oft their love and hate.
>   Phyllis! to this truth we owe
> All the love betwixt us two.
> Let not you and I inquire
> What has been our past desire;
> On what shepherds you have smiled,
> Or what nymphs I have beguiled;
> Leave it to the planets too,
> What we shall hereafter do;
> For the joys we now may prove,
> Take advice of present love.

Chernaik describes the logical structure of this poem: "The argument is a buried syllogism (containing, I might add, the fallacy of equivocation): if the present moment is the only reality, then by definition the past has neither meaning nor effect, nor has the future."[18] Probably antecedent to Andrew Marvell's more famous fallacious argument to a coy lady, "To Phyllis" proceeds first to what appears a damaging concession. If youth were to last, love would not. With disarming frankness, the invitation goes from the standard topics (time is flying) to a standard reason for ladies' coyness (the fear of lovers' fickleness), in a sort of amatory dialectic which concedes largely to the lady. But the apparent impasse opens nicely as, at line 13, the real situation between the speaker and Phyllis becomes clear: they are both recently disengaged from love affairs. The authority of the gods, in the middle of the poem, supports the value of change and leads to the conclusion that the two lovers should ignore the past and live for the moment. The extraordinary quality of the poem is in its delicacy and courtesy: "Could we (which we never can)/ Stretch our lives beyond their span." The tentative wish, in the face of unmentioned ageing and death, is quickly but with exquisite tact denied before it is fully stated. The concluding couplet reinforces the impression that the controlling principle of the poem is the persuasion of an actual lady in a real situation to submit to the poet: "For the joys we now may prove,/ Take advice of present love." The *may* defers again to the lady.

If the reader recalls Carew's "A Rapture," the persuasive delicacy of Waller's verses is put into more adequate relief. Carew begins with an abrupt announcement, "I will enjoy thee now, my Celia, come," and builds to a jolting conclusion: "Then tell me why/ This goblin Honour, which the world adores,/ Should make men atheists [in fighting duels], and not women whores." Waller begins with a polite question; and the concluding phrase, "take advice of present love," still regards the matter from the lady's viewpoint—she is thinking it over—and suggests what, in such a sensible procedure, she might consider.

In the two poems "Go, Lovely Rose" and "To a Lady in a Garden" one senses that the unnamed person addressed is different from the other, often indistinguishable, ladies of Waller's verse—Flavia, Amoret, Chloris, Sylvia, Sacharissa. This lady seems younger, gentler, shyer, more naive.

Go, Lovely Rose!

Go, lovely Rose!
Tell her that wastes her time and me
That now she knows,
When I resemble her to thee,
How sweet and fair she seems to be.

Tell her that's young,
And shuns to have her graces spied,
That hadst thou sprung
In deserts, where no men abide,
Thou must have uncommended died.

Small is the worth
Of beauty from the light retired;
Bid her come forth,
Suffer herself to be desired,
And not blush so to be admired.

Then die! that she
The common fate of all things rare
May read in thee;
How small a part of time they share
That are so wondrous sweet and fair!

The poet's message actually will transmute her naiveté, but the
rose as messenger preserves some of the gentleness; the harsh
truths are muffled since they are the experience of the rose, for
which the poet, the girl, and the reader have sympathy. The
sadness, for all three as much as for the rose, will not lead to an
overwhelming question or an assault on the gates of life but to an
enjoyment chastened by a sense of the brevity of life and
softened by communal awareness or shared nostalgia.[19]

"To a Lady in a Garden," apart from differences in tone and
melodiousness, looks like a fore-study of Marvell's "To His Coy
Mistress."

Sees not my love how time resumes
The glory which he lent these flowers?
Though none should taste of their perfumes,
Yet must they live but some few hours;
Time what we forbear devours!

> Had Helen, or the Egyptian Queen,
> Been ne'er so thrifty of their graces,
> Those beauties must at length have been
> The spoil of age, which finds out faces
> In the most retired places.
>
> Should some malignant planet bring
> A barren drought, or ceaseless shower,
> Upon the autumn or the spring,
> And spare us neither fruit nor flower;
> Winter would not stay an hour.
>
> Could the resolve of love's neglect
> Preserve you from the violation
> Of coming years, then more respect
> Were due to so divine a fashion,
> Nor would I indulge my passion.

Comparing this to Marvell's poem, the modern reader will likely regret the absence of strong, compelling images; but to understand Waller he needs to note that, from his perspective, Marvell's images are so brutal as to seem punitive rather than seductive. Even while mentioning such threats as devouring time, the spoil of age, the violation of years, the poet seems to give them the acknowledgment of casual acquaintance.

The delicacy of the poem is a mediation between the values the lady sees in retirement in a garden and the values the speaker discovers (or emphasizes rhetorically) in order to change her behavior. The main device is reference to what time does to the garden, with which the lady has identified herself. The status of time at the beginning, vis-à-vis the garden, is like that of the speaker at the end: the giver of goods. Time takes back ("resumes") the lent glory; the poet, if good could be achieved thereby, would retract his love. The lady has chosen the chaste primeval virtues of solitude in a garden; as in other poems of the sixteenth and seventeenth centuries the motive of such retirement is to avoid the mutability and decay of the world. But Waller discovers the garden to be subject to the same laws as the world. H. M. Richmond prefers an alternate title to this poem "To a Lady in Retirement," which appears in the 1645 editions but not in any later ones controlled by the poet.[20] I suspect the reason for Richmond's preference relates to an undervaluing of the third stanza, which (as I see it) is important in establishing the garden's subjection to time and chance. The garden poem draws on several Western myths. Inevitable is the recollection of Eden and the medieval-Renaissance association of the convent, the monastery, or retreat with an attempt to recapture the values of the first garden. Examples can be found in such widely separated popular expressions of Stoic-Christianity as Boethius' *Consolation* and Edward Dyer's "My Mind to Me a Kingdom Is." These are precisely the lady's models; and there is ironic acceptance of her principles in the references to Helen and Cleopatra, in stanza two. But the poem is an attack on the Stoic-Christian garden tradition by means of an appeal to an alternative archetype, the Epicurean garden, a place of elegant pleasure. The next-to-last line recalls the standard criticism of stoic "god-like " conceit and the distinction repeated by the Wife of Bath that chastity is enjoined only on those who would live perfectly. As forbearance does not prevent the fall (the inevitable loss of the beauties of the garden), then, the argument concludes, one should add pleasure to the beauty there. The lady must take what she has before it is "resumed": beauty by time and love by the poet.

The most interesting *carpe diem* poem that Waller wrote is "Of Sylvia":

> Our sighs are heard; just Heaven declares
> The sense it has of lover's cares;
> She that so far the rest outshined,
> Sylvia the fair, while she was kind,
> As if her frowns impaired her brow,
> Seems only not unhandsome now.
> So when the sky makes us endure
> A storm, itself becomes obscure.
>
> Hence 'tis that I conceal my flame,
> Hiding from Flavia's self her name,
> Lest she, provoking Heaven, should prove
> How it rewards neglected love.
> Better a thousand such as I,
> Their grief untold, should pine and die,
> Than her bright morning, overcast
> With sullen clouds, should be defaced.

This subtle poem stands in a tradition of love poems in which the lover argues that the beloved must be kind in order to be truly beautiful. Showing Waller's importance in that tradition—or rather how his poem excels in its kind—H. M. Richmond has given a brilliant explication: the poem "displays a lithe sinuosity of analysis [psychological and social] coupled with an irony as inconspicuous as the poem's intention is razor-like."[21] What Richmond admires reminds one of the serpentine cunning perceived in Waller's uncle, John Hampden; and it is from the Hampdens, according to John Aubrey, that Waller derived his gift for poetry. So there is much sense in Richmond's further suggestion that Waller extricates himself from "tangles" in love as deftly as in politics, and with more honor.

The irony of the poem inheres in the adoption almost totally of the ladies' anxiety as the ultimate concern in all real or potential relationships. The anxiety is a fear of loss of beauty, equated with rainstorms and these (heavenly frowns) in turn with ladies' expressions of disfavor. These expressions mar beauty. Thus the poet's slavish adoption of their perspective leads to an image with a counterargument: beauty can mar itself. Since such marring is as chancy as rain, the poet will do all he can not to provoke it, in Sylvia's case, in order to avoid the sad fate of the other lady.

I am tempted to add that the heavens distantly rumble through the poem, reminding us that the poet's extraordinary delicacy in *not* precipitating a loss of beauty is *not* the case in the larger dispensation. It is a "just Heaven" that punishes Sylvia (although so strong a word as *punishes* almost disharmonizes with the courtesy of the poem); it is also the natural order to render the day ugly so that storms may be endurable. The poet renders himself a true ladies' man in wishing to save Flavia from "provoking Heaven." He makes himself amiable in a touching concern for the threatenings of the natural and divine order, the stern decrees of which he like the ladies would prevent.

The strategy is to bring the lady to see that there is another alternative. She can receive the speaker with favor, returning love for love and avoiding loss of beauty. Richmond's suggestion of the parallel to Waller's escape from execution is informative, for in both cases he works his will by appealing to the fears of his audience. When he was brought to the bar of the House of Commons, he exercised the greatest ingenuity in raising the specter of further court-martial proceedings against such other members of the House as might later offend. What is remarkable in both cases is that the threat is allowed to surface only in such contexts as are most amiable and well-intentioned (or "smooth"). That is to say, the tone is skillfully maintained—a tone of concern in the one, a tone of contrition in the other.

It was Samuel Johnson's opinion that Waller's amatory poems might have an adverse moral effect by "shewing the world under a false appearance"—"so far as they obtain credit from the young and inexperienced, as misleading expectation and misguiding practice." If this means that Waller's poems might be seductive, Johnson is certainly right, but if the point is that Waller misrepresented the circumstances in love affairs, then one may appeal to experience and to Johnson's own perception, which is clear in his judgment of two of Waller's poems on matters which Johnson himself must have felt keenly: "Among Waller's little poems are some, which their excellency ought to secure from oblivion . . . *To Amoret*, comparing the different modes of regard . . . and the verses *On Love*, that begins 'Anger in hasty words or blows.'"

"To Amoret" develops a series of points of comparison between the speaker's regard for the cold Sacharissa and his feeling for the warm Amoret:

> Amoret! as sweet and good
> As the most delicious food,
> Which, but tasted, does impart
> Life and gladness to the heart.
>   Sacharissa's beauty's wine
> Which to madness doth incline;
> Such a liquor as no brain
> That is mortal can sustain.

The ingenuity of the poem consists in developing nine such points of distinction, which reveal the character and relationships of the three persons, but leave a question at the end whether the lover seriously pursues Amoret (freeing himself from Sacharissa's spell) or whether he hopes Sacharissa, overbearing, will grow warm like Amoret.

"Of Love" treats of the self-defeating state of the sensitive, courtly lover. I suspect that Johnson's high opinion of it relates to his own experience with Mrs. Porter's and other ladies' courtly prejudices: "Sir, she had read the old romances, and had got into her head the fantastical notion that a woman of spirit should use her lover like a dog."[22] The poem falls into two parts: in the first thirty-eight lines the speaker rails against the system of abject fear and devotion to ladies; in the last sixteen lines he shows that his indignation has not freed him from the slavery of love. The psychological perception is fine:

> Anger, in hasty words or blows,
> Itself discharges on our foes;
> And sorrow, too, finds some relief
> In tears, which wait upon our grief;
> So every passion, but fond love,
> Unto its own redress does move.

Women, like horses, he asserts, "(born to be controlled)/ Stoop to the forward and the bold," rather than to men so affected by love that they "fawn, and creep." Stoutly, he says the self-defeat is ridiculous and is the very opposite of the custom of the "wiser East," where the master, dealing imperiously with his harem,

> beckons to the willing dame,
> Preferred to quench his present flame;
> Behold as many gallants here,
> With modest guise and silent fear,
> All to one female idol bend,
> While her high pride does scarce descend
> To mark their follies, he would swear
> That these her guard of eunuchs were,
> And that a more majestic queen,
> Or humbler slaves, he had not seen.
>   All this with indignation spoke,
> In vain I struggled with the yoke
> Of mighty Love; that conquering look,
> When next beheld, like lightning strook
> My blasted soul, and made me bow
> Lower than those I pitied now.
>   So the tall stag, upon the brink
> Of some smooth stream about to drink,

> Surveying there his armed head,
> With shame remembers that he fled
> The scorned dogs, resolves to try
> The combat next; but if their cry
> Invades again his trembling ear,
> He straight resumes his wonted care,
> Leaves the untasted spring behind,
> And, winged with fear, outflies the wind.

The speaker's ambivalence is sharply, almost painfully realized in the movement from the contrast with the Turk to the comparison of the lover to a harried stag. The overtones of nobility and pride in the image of the stag echo the Turk's untroubled imperiousness in love, while at the same time fear of the combat he is certain to lose (the lover's unequal combat in love) dominates. The poem seems intended only to define a problem: love is a problematic emotion; the sensitive male can only suffer and flee.

The song "Peace, babbling Muse!" offers a possible solution for the lover.

> Peace, babbling Muse!
> I dare not sing what you indite;
> Her eyes refuse
> To read the passion which they write.
> She strikes my lute, but, if it sound,
> Threatens to hurl it on the ground;
> And I no less her anger dread,
> Than the poor wretch that feigns him dead,
> While some fierce lion does embrace
> His breathless corpse, and licks his face[−]
> Wrapped up in silent fear he lies,
> Torn all in pieces if he cries.

One of the realities of love is the discrepancy, created by the "nature of things" or by the courtly system, between male imperative and female resistance, or between a man's sensitivity to a woman's body and his sensitivity to her not-altogether-positive attitude about sex. (Perhaps one should add, "in the seventeenth century.") The more sensitive he is to both, the greater the conflict, as Waller shows in this song, which has an alternate title, *"Banist if he made Loue."* The poem, like many others by Waller, develops through use of an allusion to a classical myth and the suave use of two carefully polished images, which accentuate the acuteness of the conflict. The lady's physical appeal to him is like her striking a lute—but he dare not respond (make a sound). The fear he feels suggests an image of a man licked by a lion (there are overtones of cruelty in the image), when again though provoked and tormented he must make no sound. But the poet makes a sound, a poem, which suggests that the lion-lady can be tamed. And the means of the taming is the Orphic power of music or poetry.

In further friendly disagreement with Dr. Johnson, I would offer one additional poem as proof of the honesty, complexity, and morality of Waller's perception in love affairs:

Song

Chloris! farewell. I now must go;
For if with thee I longer stay,
Thy eyes prevail upon me so,
I shall prove blind, and lose my way.

Fame of thy beauty, and thy youth,
Among the rest, me hither brought;
Finding this fame fall short of truth,
Made me stay longer than I thought.

For I'm engaged by word and oath,
A servant to another's will;
Yet, for thy love, I'd forfeit both,
Could I be sure to keep it still.

But what assurance can I take,
When thou, foreknowing this abuse,
For some more worthy lover's sake,
Mayst leave me with so just excuse?

For thou mayst say, 'twas not thy fault
That thou didst thus inconstant prove;
Being by my example taught
To break thy oath, to mend thy love.

No, Chloris! no: I will return,
And raise thy story to that height,
That strangers shall at distance burn,
And she distrust me reprobate.

> Then shall my love this doubt displace,
> And gain such trust, that I may come
> And banquet sometimes on thy face,
> But make my constant meals at home.

The delight of this poem is that a lover's perplexity is solved by rhetoric (as in "Peace, babbling Muse," where the solution was by poetry), which is Waller's very own trump. And the delight is not diminished by the "moral insight."[23] The speaker is tempted to stay—blinded by beauty—but knows that if he breaks a vow and stays she will have precedent for doing the same to him, learning, as expressed in balanced oxymoron: "To break thy oath, to mend thy love." The solution is for the speaker to leave but to praise the lady "That strangers shall at distance burn"—that is, to court her through the chaste medium of poems of praise. Avoiding the dubieties of broken vows, he gains through poetry her love, in an innocent and aesthetic form whose equivalent is the enjoying, visually, of her beauty: "I may come/ And banquet sometimes on thy face,/ But make my constant meals at home." The metaphor at the end—one of two or three in a plain, late poem—returns to the value of the original attraction, the lady's beauty, and allows the maximal enjoyment consonant with the poet's standards. And the poem itself is earnest of his promised praise.

H. M. Richmond has enriched our reading of Jacobean lyrics by tracing the increase of psychological insight in seventeenth-century English poems over their analogues and prototypes. And he has made the major claim for Waller's significance in the lyric: looking at a progression of poems leading to Waller, he concludes: "Waller characteristically expresses the whole pattern with elegant beauty." The poem in question is "To Flavia."

> 'Tis not your beauty can engage
> My wary heart;
> The sun, in all his pride and rage,
> Has not that art;
> And yet he shines as bright as you,
> If brightness could our souls subdue.
>
> 'Tis not the pretty things you say,
> Nor those you write,
> Which can make Thyrsis' heart your prey;

> For that delight,
> The graces of a well-taught mind,
> In some of our own sex we find.
>
> No, Flavia! 'tis your love I fear;
> Love's surest darts,
> Those which so seldom fail him, are
> Headed with hearts;
> Their very shadows make us yield;
> Dissemble well, and win the field.

Richmond has shown that Waller's achievement appears in the clearest light when his poems are compared to the best poems in the same tradition:

One notices at once the skeptical insight of the last lines [of "To Flavia"], which show a greater awareness than Campion's poems that even psychological virtues are potentially suspect. The paradox of fearing a woman's love more than the fascination of her beauty is as beautifully weighed and poised as anything we have encountered, and the light dash of cynicism in the conclusion gives a perfect hint of astringency to the whole. Few poets can more discreetly surprise us than Waller when he warns us against the fatal attraction, not of beauty nor of wit, but of the gracious and sympathetic woman. What would Horace have made of *this* warning, one wonders . . .[24]

I would add that there is still other awareness about the situation with which Waller is playing. For one thing, the speaker places himself in what is ordinarily the woman's role: wary of would-be lovers who try to attract her by their appearance (in stanza one, note the image of the masculine sun), by their wit, and by the gift (or the feigned gift) of their hearts. Curiously, he shows himself most fearful of that which the ladies fear least—making conquests. But, *like* most ladies, he appears fearful of revealing that he loves or admires. If the real purpose of the poem is seduction (say, of a shy lady), the reversal of roles is an attempt to win by retreating, an old ploy in the battle of the sexes. I think the response which Flavia would make (or which the poem elicits) is "But I don't have to dissemble." If the poem is not an invitation to love, it intends at least to force the matter to an *éclaircissement.*

Unlike most of the Cavaliers, Waller never wrote a poem in' praise of country life. This is somewhat surprising as Waller owned a large, comfortable country estate and as we have some evidence outside his poems of his love of the countryside.[25] While some of his poems are loco-descriptive or topographical— notably "Upon His Majesty's Repairing of St. Paul's" and "On St. James's Park"—nowhere does he develop a poem around the values of country living. In neither of two poems "At Penshurst"—which allude by *title* to Jonson's vision of ordered, bountiful life in his poem "To Penshurst"—does Waller exhibit the popular Horatian, Ciceronian, or Cavalier interest in rural happiness.[26] In Waller's first "At Penshurst," the estate exists as a backdrop to the lady's beauty, responsive to it and civilized by it. In the second, which is by far the better poem, the poet's ingenuity is in using the estate to reinforce his complaint: "While in the park I sing, the listening deer/ Attend my passion, and forget to fear./ When to the beeches I report my flame,/ They bow their heads, as if they felt the same."

In this rhetorical poem, Waller takes his case against Sacharissa to the public and to the court of highest authority. He aligns himself with erotic deer and trees and gods at Penshurst, Sacharissa's country home, invokes her uncle, Sir Philip Sidney, and enlists thereby the sympathy of his polite readers, who share Sir Philip's values.[27] Sacharissa is excluded from the aureate communion:

> To no human stock
> We owe this fierce unkindness, but the rock,
> That cloven rock produced thee, by whose side
> Nature, to recompense the fatal pride
> Of such stern beauty, placed those healing springs,
> Which not more help, than that destruction, brings.

Images of flames are associated with the poet, whose orphic powers work only on himself.

> Thy heart no ruder than the rugged stone,
> I might, like Orpheus, with my numerous moan
> Melt to compassion; now, my traitorous song
> With thee conspires to do the singer wrong;
> While thus I suffer not myself to lose
> The memory of what augments my woes;
> But with my own breath still foment the fire,
> With flames as high as fancy can aspire!

Appropriately, at such a moment of Dionysian despair, Apollo (urbanely styled "the president of verse") intervenes to save his disciple. And, as I shall argue in the next chapter, the image of his going to sea may refer to his turning to more serious public themes, including several concerning the British navy. Although in the last eight lines the poet's abject hopelessness intrudes overmuch, the stoutness of his attack on Sacharissa is not undercut. The poet "from the winds and tempests does expect/ A milder fate than from her cold neglect." The abjectness is part of the courtesy, especially necessary as he, not following Apollo's advice, is writing a poetic apology of himself with the implicit principle that one who writes so well ought to attract a niece of Sir Philip Sidney. The poem is a demonstration of the lady's bad judgment.

IV   *Lyric Craft and Craftiness*

Waller's lyrics give the impression of having been easy to write. The typical effect is of simplicity, of artlessness. They are designed to persuade us that they are inevitably thus, as they are, right and easy. We hear discourse that is delicate and courteous; the communication is civilized, social, cultured in a broad or surface manner. The voices we hear, as in polite company, reveal, only with tact or with oblique or veiled reference, the most intimate and important concerns. Intimacies are not ruled out, but rather civilized into indirection and suggestion.

The themes often are precise understandings of complex relationships, usually of lovers. The speaker, the poet or his persona, exercises cunning to persuade, to create impressions, to reveal a truth. But a craft encloses his cunning, and we see in his words and purposes truths about the situation of the speaker. An ironic awareness plays around nearly every commitment, opinion, enthusiasm. Aside from ultimate insights, the gain of this mode is the preservation and representation of the several perspectives of a particular moment of a love affair. The psychological perceptivity renders vivid and exciting the ordinary and normal in the experience of lovers.

What produces the apparent artlessness is a strategy of harmonization of the poet's resources and devices. Suave ingenuity controls sound and rhyme and image (simile, metaphor, analogy) and rhetorical device (antithesis, turn, pun, paradox,

zeugma) toward, sparingly, the sharpening of subtle persuasive
or emotive points. Although nearly every poem seems written to
have a very real effect in a concrete set of circumstances, the
poet is always aware that he is using a medium which has a
tradition and elaborate resources, and which assigns to itself the
urbane modes of ironic perceptivity.

CHAPTER 3

Panegyrics

Yet let me show, a poet's of some weight,
And (though no soldier) useful to the state.
. . . .
I scarce can think him such a worthless thing,
Unless he praise some monster of a king.

(Pope, *To Augustus*)

I *Introduction*

THE actions of the most important political personalities
occasioned Waller's major panegyrical epigrams and epistles.
Although (I suppose) we may be disposed to admit all subjects to
be poetic, we hesitate to concede that a poet may *successfully*
praise Charles I, Viscount Falkland, Cromwell, Charles II, and
James II. By fate, not design, Waller's art (a gilding craft) found
exercise in the great historical actors of his century. I propose to
examine eight poems about these actors and to conclude with a
discussion of myth in the panegyric and of a theme concerning
the British navy and peace, which is developed in several poems.

II *The Major Panegyrics*

A. "Of the Danger His Majesty [Being Prince] Escaped in the Road at Saint Andrews"

Samuel Johnson said that Waller in his longer poems aimed at
dignity and greatness. Put another way, Waller sought to *give* his
subjects dignity and grandeur. He shared this goal with
contemporary poets and artists, who also found in the Stuart
imperative for aggrandizement an ongoing incentive. The
connection between reality and its ennoblement in art was

67

realized most happily in the masque, in which the king and queen themselves would act out the poet's idealizations. Thus the royal lady, complimented by the poet's representation as the queen of love, returns the compliment by *becoming* the queen of love in the representation. One wonders who is more obliged.

Some sympathy with Waller's panegyrical poems can be developed if one keeps in mind their purpose (to give dignity and greatness to the subject) and the influence of the masque. The panegyric is a masque without the spectacle, without the actual representation of action before an audience. Otherwise, it is a genre very close to the masque, with many similarities of form and substance; the masque was the poetic context out of which Waller developed his complimentary verse. If Waller's reader has just attended a masque—whether by Jonson, Beaumont and Fletcher, or Carew—he will come to the panegyric with the right expectations; the following qualities will seem to him right, inevitable: aggrandizing intentions, allusions to pagan myth, elaborate historical parallels, hyperbolic tone, and emphasis on melody. A few lines from Jonson's *Masque of Beautie* illustrate these characteristics; the passage concerns the rather improbable ordeal of four Ethiopian ladies traveling by sea to England, where they hope to be changed from black to fair:

> When Proteus, the gray *Prophet* of the Sea,
> Met them [twelve Ethiopian ladies who are now fair English
>   beauties], and made report how other four,
> Of their black kind (whereof their Sire had store)
> Faithful to that great wonder, so late done
> Upon their Sisters, by bright *Albion*
> Had followed them to seek Britania forth
> And there to hope like favor, as like worth.
> Which Night envied, as done in her despight,
> And (mad to see an Aethiope washed white)
> Thought to prevent in these, lest men should deem
> Her color, if thus changed, of small esteem.
> And so, by malice and her magic tossed
> The Nymphs at sea, as they were almost lost,
> Till, on an island they by chance arrived,
> That floated in the main; where, yet she had gived
> Them so, in charmes of darkness, as no might

> Should loose them thence but their changed
>   sisters' sight.
> Whereat the twelve [sisters] (in pity moved, and kind)
> Straight put themselves in act, the place to find.

The temporarily lost four ladies and their twelve sisters—the miraculously whitened beauties—appear near the end of the masque. In 1609 Queen Anne and noble ladies at court pleased themselves by acting the parts of the sixteen sisters.

Waller's panegyric is in the spirit of the masque. Nature and the supernatural coalesce in a fairy realm of the imagination where excess becomes a mere elegant sufficiency. All is predicated on the propriety of pleasing compliment and flattery. For example, Jonson's masque is a continuation of an earlier one, with the cast of ladies enlarged from twelve to sixteen in order that more could be pleased and flattered.

In a number of poems of the 1630s, Waller seems to have had little other motive than the gratification of the Stuart need for mythological, masque-like compliment. About Charles I he wrote the following: "Of the Danger His Majesty [Being Prince] Escaped in the Road at Saint Andrews" (of an event in 1623, written later); "Of His Majesty's Receiving the News of the Duke of Buckingham's Death" (of an event in 1628, written later); "To the King, on His Navy" (concerning events in 1635); "Upon His Majesty's Repairing of Paul's" (between 1637 and 1639). Although Waller's poems to or about Queen Henrietta cover almost the same span of years, they too were likely put into final shape in the late 1630s: "To the Queen Occasioned upon Sight of Her Majesty's Picture" (after 1625); "Of the Queen" (in the 1630s);[1] "The Apology of Sleep" (probably written before 1639); and "Puerperium" (1639–1640).[2]

Despite these compliments, Waller seems not to have enjoyed the prominence at court he was to achieve in the Restoration.[3] His only connection with the court was apparently his brother-in-law, Nathaniel Tomkins, who was Secretary to the Queen's Council. Tomkins perhaps encouraged his poetically gifted kinsman to address the monarchs in flattering verse. It thus seems likely that "Of the Danger" was written long after the event it celebrates, in order to please the queen; for it develops a condescension to feminine perspective and presents a romanticized account of Charles escaping both a storm and a marriage with the Infanta of Spain and, with a delicacy sure to please a lady, the real or imaginary nascent love between Henrietta and Charles. In a discussion of Waller's complimentary verse, Warren L. Chernaik commented specifically on this poem as, with two others, having grown "by accretion from fragments composed at various times and reflecting various circumstances . . . the patchwork construction creates problems in unity and coherence."[4]

Setting aside the question of whether manuscript evidence bears out the thesis of fragmentary development, I think it is not the poem's lack of unity, but rather the modern reader's inability to accept the integrity of this kind of poem that is the problem. Recall Elijah Fenton's response to the poem: "This Poem may serve as a model for those who intend to succeed in Panegyric; in which our Author illustrates a plain historical fact with all the graces of poetical fiction."[5] If one believes "gracing" such an event into epic is poetry, his reading is sympathetic enough to let the poem succeed on its own terms. The poem does not show lack of skill but is problematic on account of the subject and style and what I am tempted to call Baroque excess. I am reminded of John Evelyn's uncle, somewhat a failure as an architect, as the diarist confessed: "He had a large mind, but he overbuilt every thing."[6]

If Prince Charles was calm in a dangerous storm—and how un-Cavalier is the "if"—the fact could take a number of forms, including flat statements that he was unafraid. But in Waller, "Next to the power of making tempests cease,/ Was in that storm to have so calm a peace" (lines 83-84). The principle of outdoing comparisons, including equating Charles Stuart with Christ, is that too much is not enough. But the courtesy of the poem demands that the outdoing come easily and inevitably into the lines: a storm arises, the prince is threatened, the storm recalls the tempest Christ quelled. The trick is to engage the parallel neatly, as in the phrase "Next to the power." The modern reader is prone to find the easiness insufficiently redeeming and concedes only that the likely phrasing modulates the unlikely analogy.

Perhaps it is the example of Christ, available to Charles and not to pre-Christians, which enables the next application, to Aeneas, who in "Great Maro's" story "dissolves with fear" in a terrible storm. Not so Charles, whose only concern is "love's untasted joys"—having been smitten (as Waller imagines) by Henrietta Maria in France before the visit to Spain. The meanings generated by the allusions seem more designed to please a lady than a theologian. Aeneas was fearful in a storm, near the beginning of the *Aeneid,* before his passionate affair with Dido. For Charles also romance and pleasure lay ahead. But also, the allusion may be to the broken affair with the Infanta, for after *leaving* Dido Aeneas escapes another storm *without expression of fear.*

The poem has one sustained, consistent purpose, to ennoble history with the pleasing resources of poetry. To that end, Waller employs a number of the Olympian deities (Bacchus, Jove, Mars, Neptune, Thetis, Aurora, Cupid) and introduces many references to the Bible and to pagan literature. These exist in a well-contrived, smooth narrative movement with a beginning (concerning the banquet before the storm and the hieroglyphic, forecasting song about Edward IV, who also broke an engagement for love), a middle (about the storm and Charles's recollections of Henrietta), and an ending (an exultation on the Prince's escape). The style is easy and natural. The wit consists of graceful introduction of usually obvious analogies (the obviousness contributing to the easiness) in neatly turned phrases. The prince will become, the poet foresees, "Lord of the scene where now his danger lies" (162). Waller's unobtrusive control of sound and sense was to become the standard for the couplet: "the throne of Jove,/ On which the fabric of our world depends;/ One link dissolved, the whole creation ends" (168-70).

B. "Upon His Majesty's Repairing of Paul's"

"Upon His Majesty's Repairing of Paul's" is a prayer in the lull before the storm. If one accepts the dating of Brendan O Herir,[7] it was written after 1637, probably in 1639-40, when the renovation of St. Paul's had virtually ended and when the troubles with the Scots were intensifying. On the Continent, the Thirty Years War continued, a clue to English Cassandras of approaching ill. Since ship money (1634), the Scots' riot (1637), and the Solemn League and Covenant (1638), the drift of events toward a crisis was obvious to Cavaliers as well as to their enemies. The sense of impending disaster is at the heart of this poem. While the issues rage whether the English church should purify the high or low way, whether episcopacy should be replaced by presbytery, Waller creates an ambiguous if halcyon image of the king mending, not starting anew; building, not destroying. And, while both Scots and English (including Waller's kinsmen in the matter of ship money) had become openly defiant of the king, Waller yet imagines Charles as a monarch-Amphion: "Those antique minstrels sure were Charles-like kings,/ Cities their lutes, and subjects' hearts their strings,/ On which with so divine a hand they strook,/ Consent of motion from their breath they took" (15-18). Carew whistles against the same wind in his poem "In Answer to an Elegiacal Letter upon the Death of the King of Sweden":

> But let us, that in myrtle bowers sit
> Under secure shades, use the benefit
> Of peace and plenty, which the blessed hand
> Of our good king gives this obdurate land.
>
>   . . .
>
>   What though the German drum
> Bellow for freedom and revenge, the noise
> Concerns not us, nor should divert our joys;
> Nor ought the thunder of their carabins
> Drown the sweet airs of our tun'd violins.
> Believe me, friend, if their prevailing powers
> Gain them a calm security like ours,
> They'll hang their arms up on the olive bough,
> And dance and revel then, as we do now.

If Waller's poem was written in 1639, then within a year he was to deliver his speech on supply (taxation) and against innovation in the Church when Parliament was at last convened again. The speech was, Johnson said, "one of those noisy speeches which disaffection and discontent regularly dictate." Waller the member of Parliament seems at odds with Waller the courtier-poet: he attacks "pulpit law" but goes to some lengths in the 1640 speech to show that it is the king's advisors who are making *"dangerous Innovations."*

The appeal is to the tradition, to the constitution, to the fundamental laws of the realm. That which alters is the bad. In both the speech and the poem on St. Paul's there is some ambiguity in the matter of traditional authority.[8] Waller devises

a significant image from the fact of the removal of the sheds
which had been built against the cathedral:

> Those state-obscuring sheds, that like a chain
> Seemed to confine and fetter him again;
> Which the glad saint shakes off at his command,
> As once the viper from his sacred hand:
> So joys the aged oak, when we divide
> The creeping ivy from his injured side.
>   Ambition rather would affect the fame
> Of some new structure, to have borne her name.
>   . . .
>
>   an earnest of his grand design
> To frame no new church, but the old refine. (21-36)

The poem dwindles to a series of flaccid applications and
outdoing compliments, except for the epigrammatic conclusion:
"Glad, though amazed, are our neighbour kings,/ To see such
power employed in peaceful things;/ They list not urge it to the
dreadful field;/ The task is easier to destroy than build" (61-64).

Waller's images can be all things to all men: the Puritans felt
the Church was fettered, as did the Presbyterians. Does the
clearing of the sheds mean a Laudian house-cleaning or a
cleaning of Laud from the house? Or is Waller defending the
moderate Anglican establishment against both root-and-branch
absolutists—his usual position? It seems to me that he comes
very close to a significant meditation on the problem but veers
away, leaving the poetry clouded, and perhaps not even
satisfactorily representative of his own ambiguous or moderate
position. The poet wishes for a lot of things, but affirms few; he
wishes for peace, a beautifully reformed church, a king
harmonized with his kingdom, but affirms no honest policies or
clear means to these ends. The issues were too hot for statement
and the poet was unable to find or make an adequate set of
analogies or images.

It is of course not the ambiguity of the poet that flaws it.
Andrew Marvell's "An Horation Ode upon Cromwell's Return
from Ireland" is a greater poem which displays an intense
ambivalence about a related political event. But in Marvell's
poem, the tensions exist in at least a double pattern of allusion
and images (hieroglyphs, as they were sometimes called) which
convey—with irony, sympathy, and an impartiality which has

encouraged partisanship in modern critics—two forces in absolute opposition: Cromwell (and his associates) versus the executed king. Waller's poem lacks such richness of response and imaginative unity. The poem remains a faulted prayer or incantation against the coming storm.

Yet, as is often the case in Waller's life and art, his imperfection was turned to a good use. His efforts in this poem toward a reading of the hieroglyphics of royalty in harmonized couplets seem to have inspired a more consistently royalist poet, John Denham, who in *Coopers Hill* imitated (and outdid) Waller. The second known form of *Coopers Hill* and early printed versions themselves establish the reference to Waller:

> exalted I looke downe
> On Pauls, as men from thence upon the towne.
> Pauls the late theame of such a muse whose flight
> Hath bravely reacht and soar'd above thy height,
> Now shalt thou stand, though time or sword or fire
> Or zeal more feirce then they thy fall conspire,
> Secure, while thee the best of Poetts sings
> Preserv'd from ruine by the best of Kings. (11. 17-24)

Augustan criticism has linked Denham and Waller as the reformers of versification, and Johnson acquiesces in the judgment of Dryden and Pope, stating that "critical decision has given the praise of strength to Denham, and of sweetness to Waller." In an elaborate study of *Coopers Hill,* Brendan O Herir made this assessment of the use of Waller's poem to Denham: it "showed Denham how the mere existence of a grand external object could be construed as an exemplary act on its part, and one from which a pertinent lesson in political morality might be drawn."[9]

C. "To My Lord of Falkland"

Even more clearly than the poem on Paul's, "To My Lord of Falkland" is a prayer for deliverance from the approaching rebellion: "Some happy wind over the ocean blow/ This tempest yet, which frights our island so!" The organization of the poem is perfectly representative of the form of Waller's epigrams, except that it is perhaps more coherently unified than most. The first half concerns the setting forth of the elegant Earl of Holland

and the intellectual Viscount Falkland to fight against the Scots in 1639 and the danger to which Falkland has subjected himself. The second half is a series of reflections and discoveries, graced with application and metaphor, on the public context of the event. Skill lies in the management of tone, from the jaunty flattery of the foppish Holland and the poet-philosopher Falkland, to a panic fear of Falkland's being killed. The public concern, again a panic anxiety, over the approaching "tempest" is eased in the second half through optimistic analogies: an allusion to Rebecca in the book of Genesis (her sons finally reconciled) and a metaphor of a lion ceasing his self-torment and turning on his foes.

This poem is spoiled, like several others, by a consideration of the historical facts in and around it. Holland was a fool; Falkland was later to choose death in battle, deliberately "exposing that all-knowing breast"; and Waller himself was to reillustrate his hysteria in the face of death on an occasion when he might have chosen to emulate his noble friend. But the poem has some strengths. It is more personal and passionate than usual. Waller expresses a cross-section of feelings—what the normal civilized man felt at the time. And the poem makes much political sense, perhaps because it is rooted in the average man's hopes and fears, and certainly because the author understands it as both political expression and political action. It was good sense for the English to seek to placate themselves by finding a common foe, to unify at home with a war abroad. To make that action seem attractive is the poet's task. The peculiarly Wallerian touch is that the desirable vitality of reunified England is seen as growing out of its rebelliousness:

> Heaven sends, quoth I, this discord for our good,
> To warm, perhaps, but not to waste our blood;
> To raise our drooping spirits, grown the scorn
> Of our proud neighbours, who ere long shall mourn
> (Though now they joy in our expected harms)
> We had occasion to resume our arms.
>   A lion so with self-provoking smart,
> (His rebel tail scourging his noble part)
> Calls up his courage; then begins to roar
> And charge his foes, who thought him mad before.

D. "A Panegyric to My Lord Protector"

Waller's panegyrical poems are often written in the person of
one amazed—amazed at Prince Charles's courage in a storm,
King Charles I's stoicism on hearing of the death of Buckingham,
his son's patience in exile, James Duke of York's courage in
fighting the Dutch. The happy fact of "A Panegyric to My Lord
Protector" is that Cromwell *was* an amazing man, such that the
weapons in Waller's poetical arsenal find a real target. (As G. K.
Chesterton's poet Gabriel Syme says of poetry, "The rare,
strange thing is to hit the mark.") The opening lines set the
rhetorical pattern for the entire poem, a construction of
reconciled oppositions in the figures of antithesis, paradox, turn,
oxymoron, zeugma: "While with a strong and yet a gentle hand,/
You bridle faction, and our hearts command,/ Protect us from
ourselves, and from the foe,/Make us unite, and make us conquer
too." Antithesis and hint of paradox occur in each line, almost as
principles of construction: e.g., the opposition/combination of
bridling faction and commanding hearts in line 2. The other basic
rhetorical devices appear in the same four lines: zeugma in the
giving of double objects to *protect us from* in line 3; oxymoron in
strong and *gentle* of line 1; and turn, with the usual effect of
emphasis, in the repetition of *make us* in line 4. Whereas in the
lyrics Waller gracefully illuminated aspects of love with the
same figures of speech, he was unfortunate in the Stuart poems in
never having topics of praise equal to the colors of his rhetoric;
and, as Chernaik points out, his panegyric with its effects of
exaggerated image and constrained language suggested or
inspired a more successful poetic mode in the mock-heroic.[10]

In the best verse—and "A Panegyric" is Waller's best long
poem and together with some twenty songs and lyrical epigrams
will continue to attract readers and escape oblivion—in such
verse, the categories of mind or wit coalesce with what the
reader accepts as reality: a zeugma holds a lover's ambiguous
feelings, a paradox reveals the essential truth in a bewildering
event, a pun discovers a hidden connection. The categories of
mind open up the experienced world.

Viewed skeptically, remarkable poetry (especially poetry
which sets out to "grace" history) occurs when there is a
convincing overlap of rhetoric and the evidence of reality. In this
case, Cromwell was a ferocious warrior and an amiable man; he

could outfight and forgive his enemies. He was a squire with modest holdings who became the ruler of three nations and a good part of the sea.

Waller's experience of the man's nature was firsthand. They served together in the House of Commons. Waller's mother's brother married a Cromwell, who was Oliver's aunt. The same brother had a famous son, John Hampden. An unattested tradition has it that Cromwell saved Waller from execution in 1644; and it is fact that he did arrange (probably at the instigation of Waller's brother-in-law Adrian Scroope) for the pardon in 1651 which allowed the poet to return the next year to England. It is therefore likely that "A Panegyric" expresses sincere gratitude. After it was written, Cromwell sent a letter to Waller which is at least on the surface amiable and modest — and entirely consistent with his orders to his portrait painters to depict his features as they were, warts and all. In 1655 Cromwell appointed Waller to the Council of Trade and in 1656 might have been responsible for a government order to officials in Buckinghamshire to cease harassing Waller.

"A Panegyric" has at least three purposes: (1) to express, indirectly, the poet's gratitude; (2) to reinforce in Cromwell his pacific virtues; and (3) to convince the English of the justice of Cromwell's claim to rule.[11] The first takes the form, not emphasized until the end, of a celebration of heroic deeds. The second and third are sustained in a set of reconciliations — in the second, of the martial versus the irenic nature of Cromwell — in the third, of two forms of legitimating and justification of his rule, the Hobbesian versus the traditional.

As a communication to Cromwell, the poem presents a theme of his greatness in powerful peacefulness or of his peace-creating power at home and abroad. The genre itself strongly suggests the irenic theme, for the classical model is Horace's epistle "To Augustus," the emperor of peace. Cromwell himself is the pattern of his effect in the world, the accommodating of potency to order: "Oft have we wondered how you hid in peace/ A mind proportioned to such things as these;/ How such a ruling spirit you could restrain,/ And practise first over yourself to reign" (129–32). The turn and paradox of these lines are part of a recurrent rhetorical strategy whereby the theme of *concors-discordia* elaborates. In the beginning lines, quoted above, the pattern establishes itself — from the very first line, with the

reference to Cromwell's "strong, and yet a gentle hand." The
antithesis established enables Waller to emphasize one sense of
the title of "protector" (line 32)—that is, one who uses power to
defend the weak.[12] In the same context, the poet imagines the
"oppressed" of the world seeking Cromwell's help (29-30).

Although Waller indulges his habit of "outdoing" comparisons
as in the Stuart poems, these hit off sparks of truth and
contribute to a unified rhetorical and thematic effect. "When for
more worlds the Macedonian cried,/ He wist not Thetis in her lap
did hide/ Another yet; a world reserved for you,/ To make more
great than that he did subdue" (72-76). Mighty like Alexander,
Cromwell has found both the lamented other world *and* a
greater thing to accomplish. The crucial example of his
competence in war and peace is in the case of the Scots. Once
provoked by Laud and Charles, the Scots became a problem
such that Charles could neither successfully oppose them nor
unite with them; he spent a decade failing. Emphatic, decisive, is
Waller's point that Cromwell subdued the Scots and brought
them into harmony with the rest of the island. Cromwell's
wisdom in his policy of ready accommodation with his former
enemies is given point by elegant antithesis, paradox, and
application: "Preferred by conquest, happily o'erthrown,/ Falling they rise, to be with us made one;/ So kind dictators made,
when they came home,/ Their vanquished foes free citizens of
Rome" (93-96).

When this rhetorical pattern becomes most dense, Waller uses
an image of animal fierceness, one of the few images of the poem
(nearly all of which have to do with terrible or divisible forces in
nature):

> Your never-failing sword made war to cease;
> And now you heal us with the arts of peace;
> Our minds with bounty and with awe engage,
> Invite affection, and restrain our rage.
>
> Less pleasure take brave minds in battles won,
> Than in restoring such as are undone;
> Tigers have courage, and the rugged bear,
> But man alone can, whom he conquers, spare.
>
> To pardon willing, and to punish loath,
> You strike with one hand, but you heal with both;

> Lifting up all that prostrate lie, you grieve
> You cannot make the dead again to live.
>
> When fate, or error, had our age misled,
> And o'er these nations such confusion spread,
> The only cure, which could from Heaven come down,
> Was so much power and clemency in one! (109-124)

Because of Waller's reputation as a sycophantic poet, it is necessary to set special emphasis on lines in which he tells home truths, however obliquely. Cromwell had a large share in leading the parliamentary forces until the king was executed and the realm in a state of chaos. In finding the good in Cromwell's usurpation, Waller does not gloss over the bad, in lines which imply Cromwell's resemblance to Brutus:

> But living virtue, all achievements past,
> Meets envy still, to grapple with at last.
>
> This Caesar found; and that ungrateful age,
> With losing him fell back to blood and rage;
> Mistaken Brutus thought to break their yoke,
> But cut the bond of union with that stroke.
> . . .
> As the vexed world, to find repose, at last
> Itself into Augustus' arms did cast;
> So England now does, with like toil oppressed,
> Her weary head upon your bosom rest. (147-172)

At the concluding edge of the pattern, Waller uses the technique of *praeterito*.[13] Denying he will praise Cromwell's military achievements, he elaborates the praise in the denial and the poem closes with the poet bringing to Cromwell both "bays and olive"—symbols of triumph and peace. Curiously, in so many kinds of praise, there is no mention of Cromwell's sense of religious mission, as Waller apparently again looked on political matters with a "carnal eye."[14] I do not experience in the poem Waller's "drawing on the double tradition of messianic-imperial prophecy, biblical and Roman" nor his presenting much of a Christian motif.[15] Nor can I accept the Tertullianism of a critical habit which praises a thing because it is Christian: *amo quia Christianum.* The applications or allusions are largely from and to Greek and Roman history and mythology, a favorite topic of

Waller and Cromwell's conversation, according to the 1711 *Life*.[16] Two applications are from the Bible. David's "humble" life before he replaced Saul is applied to the quietness of Cromwell while yet his "princely virtues slept" (135–36). Joseph's dream of his brothers' bowing to him is analogous to the nations' paying homage to Cromwell. As I shall argue later, it is noteworthy that both David and Joseph replaced, actually or virtually, the ruling monarchs of a realm. The applications from ancient "story" have several functions. They convey direct compliment—Cromwell is "our Mars" (176)—or are at the heart of an "outdoing" comparison: Rome *walled* but Cromwell *beat* the Scots (85). The predominating Roman allusions ennoble the irenic theme of the poem, authenticating the English experience as instance of classical or general or "uniformitarian" truths—Neptune calming the seas that raged against Aeneas (9), Rome's receiving conquered foes as citizens (96), Augustus bringing an era of peace (168–72).

Waller uses few images; these have a quality of simile, since the analogy is usually so clearly presented.[17] The most noticeable images in the "Panegyric," six in number, are drawn from mainly chaotic, confused, or fierce natural forces. Those who oppose Cromwell are made to prefer such liberty as obtains when all "Without control upon their fellows prey" (8); Cromwell, like Neptune, repressed the "storms of ambition" (12); unlike tigers and bears, man (i.e., Cromwell) conquers and forgives; and the parliamentary armies are controlled, like a lion, by the original tamer (165–68). Two complex images, the heart of the meaning in the poem, work together. The sun functions as vehicle for Cromwell, but also, surprisingly, for the dead king; while the stars, competing lights, are analogous to those who struggled for power after the king's death:

> Still as you rise, the state, exalted too,
> Finds no distemper while 'tis changed by you;
> Changed like the world's great scene! when, without noise,
> The rising sun night's vulgar lights destroys.
>
> Had you, some ages past, this race of glory
> Run, with amazement we should read your story;
> But living virtue, all achievements past,
> Meets envy still, to grapple with at last.

> This Caesar found; and that ungrateful age,
> With losing him fell back to blood and rage;
> Mistaken Brutus thought to break their yoke,
> But cut the bond of union with that stroke.
>
> That sun once set, a thousand meaner stars
> Gave a dim light to violence, and wars,
> To such a tempest as now threatens all,
> Did not your mighty arm prevent the fall. (141-56)

Although these lines are otherwise significant, they are part of a sustained theme of the use of power to subdue forces of savagery and chaos.

Less obvious and more important than the praise or the rein-forcement of Cromwell's peaceful and forgiving nature is the purpose to persuade the English—including the *now dissident* royalists—to accept Cromwell's reign as legitimate. Of course, his irenic nature is important in the claim and as a model for all relationships (including the royalists'): win and forgive, lose and accept. But is the rule of Cromwell legitimate because of his conquest and the fact of his present power? Does Waller borrow the reasoning of his friend and great contemporary, Thomas Hobbes?

A commonwealth by acquisition is that, where the sovereign power is acquired by force. . . . And this kind of dominion, or sovereignty, differeth from sovereignty by institution, only in this, that men who choose their sovereign, do it for fear of one another, and not of him whom they institute: but in this case, they subject themselves, to him they are afraid of. . . . But the rights and consequences of sovereignty, are the same in both. . . . And this dominion is then acquired by the victor, when the vanquished, to avoid the present stroke of death, covenanteth either in express words, or by other sufficient signs of the will, that so long as his life, and the liberty of his body is allowed him, the victor shall have the use thereof, at his pleasure. . . . It is not therefore the victory, that giveth the right of dominion over the vanquished, but his own covenant. Nor is he obliged because he is conquered; that is to say, beaten, and taken, or put to flight; but because he cometh in, and submitteth to the victor.[18]

Or preferring the older understanding in the tradition of natural law, does Waller pronounce the rule of Cromwell just because he is the most kingly man in the country, the most deserving, the most virtuous?

The assumptions of the poem seem at first glance altogether Hobbesian. The major idea, and a strong image, in the *Leviathan* is that proud, quarrelsome, dangerous beings (men) must be intimidated into peace by the authority of power, by the mighty beast the Leviathan, or the state, which tames the proud. As noted earlier, Waller gives emphasis to Cromwell's effect on the ambitious, those "thousand meaner stars" who "Gave a dim light to violence, and wars" (153-54) after Charles's sun had set. The time of violence is of course the Civil War, a condition much like that Hobbes described as the "state of nature"—a war of all against all, where life is "poor, nasty, brutish, and short." The chief inconvenience of the state of nature is the continual fear of violent death, itself the greatest evil. Fear of this evil drives men into civil societies, where all give up their liberty of doing as they like for the privilege of living secure against the violence of others. Any civil state is therefore better than the state of nature (or war); the only alternative to the civil state is anarchy. Man is civilized by fear of the power of the central authority. Hobbes's doctrines grew out of the Civil War, and he, proud to have been one of the first who ran, was true to his own doctrine about the status of fear in human choices. Fear brings man to accept the laws of nature, the primary being the obligation of all men to seek peace. By the standards of the *Leviathan,* it was wrong to rebel against Charles; the rebellion was a return to the state of nature (of war), as the chaotic years 1642-50 seem to demonstrate; Cromwell's authority is necessary and therefore justified to end the chaos and restore order and safety.

Waller seems to argue exactly as Hobbes. He quietly raises a specter of fear of further struggles in the early stanzas. Cromwell appears as having lessened anxieties and achieved goals common to all, including the royalists—"Your drooping country, torn with civil hate,/ Restored by you, is made a glorious state" (13-14). His reestablishment of naval power afforded protection from enemies abroad, reduced piracy at sea, and enabled England to become a *commercially* magical island (16-64).[19]

> Our little world, the image of the great,
> Like that, amidst the boundless ocean set,

> Of her own growth has all that Nature craves;
> And all that's rare, as tribute from the waves.
> . . .
>
> To dig for wealth we weary not our limbs;
> Gold, though the heaviest metal, hither swims;
> Ours is the harvest where the Indians mow;
> We plough the deep, and reap what others sow. (49-52, 61-64)

Most important, Cromwell solved the problem of the Scots—by conquering them and uniting with them—and he defeated the Irish and the Dutch. The first 124 lines present Cromwell as the restorer of English tranquility.

Thus far the assumptions of the poem are politically realistic or positivistic, in the manner of Hobbes and Machiavelli, the crucial issues being the success of the government in controlling its people and defeating its neighbors. The tradition that Machiavelli and Hobbes opposed was common and still strong in Waller's day, and his appeal to the understanding of justice as natural law may have been genuinely felt—or used merely for persuasive effect. It is ambiguous whether Waller expressed himself or his audience. In either case, his culture, especially in poems of idealizing praise, maintained the natural law which teaches that justice is the rule of the best, those most qualified by wisdom and virtue. The prevalence of this view appears most graphically in praise of hereditary monarchs, whose title to rule is birth, but to whom all virtues are poetically attributed, lending the authority of natural justice to the fact of authority based on convention. The problem arose from time to time, however, that those who rule are not the worthiest; they are in fact often stupid, incompetent, or corrupt.

Synthesizing or collapsing the Hobbesian and the traditional understanding, Waller slyly bases Cromwell's claim, as against Charles I's, on the judgment that Cromwell has control and that he is the better man. Ruler *de facto* and *de jure,* Cromwell has power and virtue ("living virtue", 147). I am not now proposing Waller's ultimate agreement or disagreement with Hobbes, nor his using Hobbes's views on the natural-law tradition merely for rhetorical purposes. He obviously wishes to make a strong case with wide appeal, and it is clear that after line sixty-four the poem takes on more and more assumptions of natural justice to

legitimate Cromwell's rule. The middle section is devoted to
Cromwell's solution of the problem of the Scots (and the Irish
and the Dutch). As Waller (and others) saw it, Charles baited the
Scots and precipitated the struggle with parliament and the Civil
War.[20] Defeated in 1639 and saddled with a Scots army to bribe,
he was forced to convene the parliament. The Scots then entered
English affairs to work (especially from the royalist point of
view) great mischief—until Cromwell defeated them in 1648
and 1650. The central point of Waller's poem is that Cromwell
corrected Charles's errors and succeeded where Charles failed.

In the rest of the poem (125-188), Waller uses his favorite
poetical tools to justify Cromwell's claim to rule. The prototype
of Cromwell's harmonized regime is his own self-control
(129-32). An allusion elevates the modest achievements of his
early career: "Born to command, your princely virtues slept,/
Like humble David's, while the flock he kept" (135-36). Once in
the public arena "Your flaming courage, and your matchless
worth,/ Dazzling the eyes of all that did pretend,/ To fierce
contention gave a prosperous end" (138-40). The image of light,
illustrative of natural worth, transforms into the sun, the symbol
of kingship, but with a specific connotation emphasized: "Still as
you rise, the state, exalted too,/ Finds no distemper while 'tis
changed by you;/Changed like the world's great scene! When,
without noise,/ The rising sun night's vulgar light destroys"
(141-44). That is, his inevitable authority ended the disorder
created by the rebels. At this point Waller seems to digress on
the theme of the resistance of ambitious, less worthy men to
"living virtue" (147), as Caesar himself had discovered: "and that
ungrateful age,/ With losing him fell back to blood and rage;/
Mistaken Brutus thought to break their yoke,/ But cut the bond
of union with that stroke" (149-52).

The effect of one bold flash in so much politeness is one of
sudden, unavoidable irony (something like the force of truth
presupposed in the adage, "murder will out"). The description of
Caesar as "living virtue" comes close to a reprehension of
Cromwell but in fact discovers a reason for royalists to support
him: he is alive and competent. What Waller achieves is a yoking
of Charles and Cromwell in the application of Caesar (both
opposed by lesser, envious, ambitious men). The reference to
Brutus, immediately thereafter (151), puts the two into the
opposition that a royalist would prefer, with the emphasis on a

murder which creates civil disorder. But the final Roman association is Augustus: "As the vexed world, to find repose, at last/ Itself into Augustus' arms did cast" (169-70). Collapsing Cromwell into three associations, Caesar-Brutus-Augustus, enables Waller to speak accurately and persuasively. While it is true Cromwell caused disorder, he was soon, like Charles, opposed by an ambitious assembly and was, like Augustus, the restorer of peace and order. The intent of the Roman applications is to force a royalist who is antagonistic to Cromwell to see himself as being like those who attacked Charles.

Waller returns to the sun image to elaborate the connection between Charles and Caesar: "That sun once set, a thousand meaner stars/ Gave a dim light to violence, and wars,/ To such a tempest as now threatens all,/ Did not your mighty arm prevent the fall" (153-56). Here Charles is the setting sun; and this setting produced a competitive Hobbesian state of nature (of war), a night of rival stars, which are eclipsed by the rising sun. The image of the beneficent greater light fuses the Hobbesian and the traditional values; the contrast between rising and setting reemphasizes Cromwell's merit as opposed to Charles's.

As noted earlier in the discussion of "To My Lord of Falkland," Waller was unable to create a work that held polarities in an unified opposition. In this respect that poem was compared unfavorably to Marvell's "Horatian Ode." In the panegyric on Cromwell, it seems that Waller, too, is able to represent an understanding, which, in striking allusion and images, does display in fascinating torsion a set of ambivalences (which is sometimes thought to be the essence of poetry). In this case, and Marvell's, the display is of the poet's insight into the complexities of real events. The utility of the poet's resources—paradox, antithesis, ambiguity—is in capturing the truth about events. Waller's poem, also, maintains a clear and persistent goal of persuasion.

The final third of the poem works by application (or allusion) its threefold purpose of praise, exhortation, and justification. This section begins with the comparison of Cromwell to David[21] and ends with an allusion to Joseph. The two enclose and support an argument for Cromwell's worthiness to replace an anointed king. The appositeness of reference to David's career is obvious; as Dryden was to say more wittily: "Tis after God's own heart to cheat an heir." And Joseph, on the basis of virtue alone, became ruler of Egypt. With self-control, foresight, competence, Joseph the provider is the biblical example of just deserts, of the success of natural justice in the conventional world. Joseph is the self-made man, who achieves not by birth but by virtue, barred in Egypt from seeking power by conventional means. The final note of the poem harmonizes the conqueror (nations bowing to him) with the provider, the man whose worth qualifies him to rule.

E. "Of a War with Spain, and a Fight at Sea"

In many ways, "Of a War with Spain, and a Fight at Sea" is Waller's most moving and humane poem, a baroque meditation on war, gold, and virtue. The poet looks at an event and in its hieroglyphics discovers the latent significations. The event is a minor British victory, taken for granted since Britain ruled the seas; there is little tension or doubt as to the outcome, and the theme is *not* England's or Cromwell's military excellence. The poem begins with reflections and smooth wordplay on the uses of Spanish gold:

> From the new world her silver and her gold
> Came, like a tempest, to confound the old;
> Feeding with these the bribed Electors' hopes,
> Alone she gave us emperors and popes;
> With these accomplishing her vast designs,
> Europe was shaken with her Indian mines. (7-12)

It ends with the suggestion that the gold captured by the English be melted down and made into a crown and scepter for Cromwell.

It is a poem of transformations. Spanish pride has altered the ordinary course of nature, in their mercantilistic imperialism, making "the sun shine on half the world in vain" (1-2). In the pun on "Indian mines" (12), Waller discovers another metamorphosis: the *mines* of ore became *bombs* in Spanish manipulations of European politics. However, because of the strength of the British navy, Spanish hegemony at sea transmutes to English (19-24). Waller works an antithesis (road-abode) into metonymy (oaks for ships), which, taken literally, has oaks growing again, at sea:

> Others may use the ocean as their road,
> Only the English make it their abode,
> Whose ready sails with every wind can fly,
> And make a covenant with the inconstant sky;
> Our oaks secure, as if they there took root,
> We tread on billows with a steady foot. (25-30)

The fight itself is precipitated by the ironically twisted signal which the Spanish galleons, nearing home, gave "To tell their joy, or to invite a barge" (38). But that signal is their death knell, for, by chance, the British ships were nearby. The poet gives a grisly picture of war at sea and digresses on the topic of man's altering for the worse the natural terrors of sailing:

> Bold were the men which on the ocean first
> Spread their new sails, when shipwreck was the worst;
> More danger now from man alone we find
> Than from the rocks, the billows, or the wind.
> They that had sailed from near the Antarctic Pole,
> Their treasures safe, and all their vessels whole,
> In sight of their dear country ruined be,
> Without the guilt of either rock or sea!
> What they would spare, our fiercer art destroys,
> Surpassing storms in terror and in noise. (51-60)

There is a certain fruitlessness in such puissance, for, as the poet reveals (in a rhetorical turn on digging and burying), nature returns the treasure to its original, hidden state:

> Vain man! whose rage buries as low that store,
> As avarice had digged for it before;
> What earth, in her dark bowels, could not keep
> From greedy hands, lies safer in the deep,
> Where Thetis kindly does from mortals hide
> Those seeds of luxury, debate, and pride. (69-74)

In his treatment of the action, the poet dwells on the nobility of the enemy Marquis, who dies by "his burning lady's side" in the midst of treasure.

> Spices and gums about them melting fry,
> And, phoenix-like, in that rich nest they die;

> Alive, in flames of equal love they burned,
> And now together are to ashes turned;
> Ashes! more worth than all their funeral cost,
> Than the huge treasure which was with them lost. (83–88)

As it emerges that the real treasure on the ship is the virtue of the Marquis and his wife, the anger of the English is transformed into kindly concern:

> These dying lovers, and their floating sons,
> Suspend the fight, and silence all our guns;
> Beauty and youth about to perish, finds
> Such noble pity in brave English minds,
> That (the rich spoil forgot, their valour's prize)
> All labour now to save their enemies.
> How frail our passions! how soon changed are
> Our wrath and fury to a friendly care!
> They that but now for honour, and for plate,
> Made the sea blush with blood, resign their hate;
> And, their young foes endeavouring to retrieve,
> With greater hazard than they fought, they dive. (89–100)

The poem is about the achievement of value through the transformation of lesser things into higher. The subject, in connection with gold, inevitably suggests the image of alchemical change of base metals. That which the Spanish took from the Indies is taken from them by the English; gold that would have made emperors and popes becomes a crown for the arch-protestant regicide Cromwell, the red-cross knight (cf. line 23). The value in the crown is that it will, in Waller's alchemical term, "fix" the state—that is, render it permanent and stable. The fight, and war generally, like the despoiling of the Indies, alters the world for the worse, but out of war comes the nobility of the valiant. Phoenix-like, baser things become golden, especially in the poet's alembic. And that metamorphosis works to change the hearts of the fierce enemy: the destroyer becomes the preserver.

I think Waller saw in the alchemy of the Marquis an image of the Civil War and the death of Charles I. He and many on both sides died bravely, and in their dying won the admiration of their enemies. The poem affirms British tradition by transforming old antagonisms so that the golden on all sides is preserved. The poet becomes almost perfectly objective about the situation, the fight

at sea, and the civil war which it seems to emblematize. The
British defeat the Spanish because they have the heavier
currency ("And knowing well that empire must decline,/ Whose
chief support and sinews are of coin,/ Our nation's solid virtue did
oppose" — 15-17); or, metaphorically, the Roundheads beat the
Cavaliers, for the same reason. The golden transmutation in the
war was, as another poet states it, that a beauty was born, the
nobility of both the valiant and the sympathy and respect of their
enemies. In a study of the variant texts, P. R. Wikeland has
argued that the poem is a "panegyrical triptych" consisting of
sections on the Marquis, the English sailors, and the English
people: "In each of these three, by a present or promised act, a
tradition is subscribed to and sustained: in the marques the
tradition of romantic love, in the sailors the Christian ethical
tradition, in the English people their constitutional traditions."[22]
I would add that the "fixing" of the state in Cromwell's golden
crown and scepter completes the alchemical changes whereby
the traditions of English monarchy, English valor, and English
generosity are transmuted by one (Cromwell) who, like fire, is
both destroyer and preserver.

The moral tone of the poem is Waller's most somber and
profound and is more on the model of the medieval themes of the
wheel of fortune and *de contemptu mundi* than anything else he
wrote. The vanity of life, the tears of things, the ironies and
paradoxes of human efforts — all figure in a texture that recreates
the experience of human gentleness surrounded by the destruc-
tion of war (as in the *Iliad* when Hector says farewell to
Andromache and frightens his son with his helmet). Finally,
although it is a poem of transformation, some things are not
changed at all — like gold, which whether Spanish or English is
regal; like virtue, whether it is in friend or foe, Cavalier or
Roundhead; and like the traditions of British civilization.

F.   "To the King, Upon his Majesty's Happy Return"

The poem on Cromwell's death, in Thorn-Drury's edition,
faces the title and first seven lines of "To the King Upon His
Majesty's Happy Return." The impression of such a juxtaposition
is, perhaps not unfairly, one of nimbleness in flattery. Waller
celebrates Charles II's return in images of the reappearance of
the sun, presumably after a time of darkness, tempest, and

winter. As Earl Miner has pointed out, the Cavaliers experienced
the mid-century troubles as a season of bad weather to be lived
through in retirement or exile.[23] Curiously, Waller assumes the
same metaphor to discover the *good* aspects of Charles's long
absence and return to a people grown weary of other alterna-
tives:

> The rising sun complies with our weak sight,
> First gilds the clouds, then shows his globe of light
> At such a distance from our eyes, as though
> He knew what harm his hasty beams would do.
>   But your full majesty at once breaks forth
> In the meridian of your reign. Your worth,
> Your mouth, and all the splendour of your state,
> (Wrapped up, till now, in clouds of adverse fate!)
> With such a flood of light invade our eyes,
> And our spread hearts with so great joy surprise. (1-10)

The sun's initial concern about harming others is of course the
right touch, for Waller thereby makes graceful obeisance while
magnifying the kindness of the powerful sun. If (as some have
said) this is abject, it is at least cunningly abject.

However, the major ideas generated in the sustained imagery
of the sun are not ones that Charles might have chosen to hear.
Waller's Pollyanna muse found the happy ideas in Charles's exile
and return. Kept from his throne so long, Charles begins in full
bloom; he will amaze the European rulers who had known him
only in his naked exile, as Waller demonstrates in a delightful
application which fuses outdoing praise with Caroline erotic
flattery:

> Princes that saw you, different passions prove,
> For now they dread the object of their love;
> Nor without envy can behold his height,
> Whose conversation was their late delight.
> So Semele, contented with the rape
> Of Jove disguised in a mortal shape,
> When she beheld his hands with lightning filled,
> And his bright rays, was with amazement killed. (29-36)

Further, Charles's travels have enabled him to mature his
judgment: "We have you now with ruling wisdom fraught,/ Nor

such as books, but such as practice, taught" (45–46). To beguile
Charles from the corollary that he was immature in 1649, Waller
adds the gilding analogy: "So the lost sun, while least by us
enjoyed,/ Is the whole night for our concern employed;/ He
ripens spices, fruits, and precious gums,/ Which from remotest
regions hither comes" (47–50).

Reminiscent of a Falstaffian argument to Prince Hal is Waller's
justification of the king's suffering: "Rude Indians, torturing all
the royal race,/ Him with the throne and dear-bought sceptre
grace/ That suffers best. What region could be found,/ Where
your heroic head had not been crowned?" (95–98). The
exhortations of the poem, with the colors of rhetoric washed out,
are not mindless compliment so much as "putting in mind of
duty." Most courteously, of course, Waller advises: forgive, but
not too quickly; look on the happy side of your exile; note that
your old opponents, the army and the navy, brought you back, as
did the people who "break forth" to demand your return (the
phrase echoes the earlier mention of the king's "breaking forth,"
line 5); continue your delicate touch in unraveling tangled
political knots; attribute your return to Providence; forgive, like
Christ, the frail; and be aware that your next great test is how
you manage in *good* fortune. The last oracular suggestion
pronounces a kind of doom on the Stuarts, that they are so much
more admirable in adversity than in prosperity, that their cause
wins men's hearts best when it is lost.

The last lines carry the imagery of the sun into the realm of
poetry, where Charles assumes the aspect of Apollo: "But, above
all, the Muse-inspired train/ Triumph, and raise their drooping
heads again!/ Kind Heaven at once has, in your person, sent/
Their sacred judge, their guard, and argument" (117–20). That
Waller should give so much authority in poetry to Charles adds
piquancy to an anecdote noted in Chapter 1: "The king, having
read the verses, reproached him for having made better ones for
Cromwell. Waller said to him, 'Sir, we poets succeed better in
fiction than in truth.'"

G. "On St. James's Park"

Professor Earl Miner has written persuasively of the excellence and significance of "On St. James's Park," as a poem about
the harmonizing good Charles II does or can do elaborated in

powerful mythic images of *discordia concors,* of the loss and regaining of paradise, of the redeemer: "The version of the Park as microcosm of the world improved by the King absorbs the other versions, because they are part of the larger world: the gallants and ladies gathering socially, the natural scene . . ., the mythical suggestions (with their emblems of harmony), and the minglings of the natural and human, of art and nature. That larger meaning of the Park as the regal world made into a paradise regained is, in one sense, a meaning led up to with great ease by the sequence of repeated and merging versions of lesser kinds."[24] If the mythical suggestions associated around the regaining of paradise are taken as the earnest center of meaning, one wonders then how Waller, sobered by twenty years of experience with enthusiasts who intended to make England another Eden, could have left the real world for so gnostic a garden.[25] The poem begins with extreme claims, one rather direct for the king, another more indirect for the poet: "Of the first Paradise there's nothing found;/ Plants set by Heaven are vanished, and the ground;/ Yet the description lasts; who knows the fate/ Of lines that shall this paradise relate?" (1–4). The excess of statement here is clearer if one recalls Waller's more sensible lines in "Of English Verse"—"Poets may boast, as safely vain,/ Their works shall with the world remain;/ Both, bound together, live or die,/ The verses and the prophecy."

The movement of "On St. James's Park" is the elevation of Charles as the creator and redeemer. He creates another Eden, this park, and also a river for it. A meteor, observed in London soon after the birth of Charles, becomes the poet's emblem of his divine redemptive and conciliatory powers: Charles reflects "On what the world may from that star expect/ Which as his birth appeared, to let us see/ Day, for his sake, could with the night agree" (127–30). Except for the hope inspired by Charles's return, the associations do not agree with many, if any, of the facts: Stuart behavior, Charles's behavior, even Waller's record in the House of Commons (where he sometimes voted and spoke against the wishes of the king and his ministers). The reader who recalls the historical facts thinks that the poet cannot be serious—here the seventeenth and eighteenth centuries experienced Waller's "insincerity"—and the imaginative frame does not enable the mythic to preclude our skeptical analysis. The lines of direct and graceful statement of myth have the force of the maxim "the king can do not wrong" as explained by David Ogg: "This . . . imposed on the subject the requirement of finding out or testing the legality of the sovereign's commands, while absolving the crown from the duty of ascertaining whether they were legal before enunciating them; in a sense therefore this interpretation of the maxim amounted to no more than this, that everyone, except the king, is supposed to know the whole law of England."[26] Perhaps, in Waller's poem, everyone but the king was supposed to know that his was only a comet and not the star of Bethlehem and to remember that millenarian expectations were only Puritan dreams.

Put another way, whereas Waller's poem on Cromwell is supported by the confirmation of its judgment from so many diverse points of view, "On St. James's Park" lacks just that. Its hopefulness bubbles over into excessive mythic parallels, all too characteristic of the agreeableness of the poet, so supple in points of courtesy before ladies and great men: "he once said, he would have given all his own Poems to have been the Author of that which my Lady Newcastle writ on a stag: And that being tax'd for this Insincerity by one of his friends, he answer'd, that he could do no less in Gallantry than be willing to devote all his own Papers to save the Reputation of a Lady, and keep her from the Disgrace of having written so ill."[27] A political illustration of this trait of Waller's character and writing occurs in a letter he wrote to Hobbes during the Protectorate, at a time when the government was imposing very strict military controls. Waller's sentiments, which surely pleased Hobbes and would have had the same effect on Cromwell, have appeared to a modern editor as "something of a surprise from one who had suffered imprisonment, heavy fine, and long exile for his royalism." In the letter, Waller wrote, "To me it seems that his Highnes [Cromwell] (who sees a good way before him) had layd sometyme since a perfect foundation of government; I mean by the Major-Generals reducing us to provences and ruling us by those provincials with the newe Levied Army."[28] Waller as a young man once heard a time-serving bishop tell James I that the king was "the Breath of our Nostrils."[29] This kind of sacrilege is perhaps as corruptive of language as of religion, and Waller may have participated in the corruption. The unfortunate tendency in some of his verse is not that it becomes, in Chernaik's phrase, mindless song, but rather mindless compliment.

In a poem embellishing history, there is always an appeal from poetry to the truth (or to the evidence). One can admire "On St. James's Park" as a well-made poem. But the reader in possession of a few facts of Stuart political history will find his admiration undercut by the excessive distance between poetic myth and reality. Earl Miner neatly assesses the poem's intricacy and success of design; Waller manages with grace and skill the major theme of Charles's harmonizing power. But the excess intrudes: the godlike Charles has an arm like a rifle; he throws a ball, which "such a fury from his arm has got,/ As from a smoking culverin 'twere shot" (65-66).

Mindless compliment may cloak, however, the cunning of a poet who ventures an intelligent admonition. Behind the appeals to Charles's notions of divine right and sun-king authority, behind grand concessions to his love of erotic ambles and other outdoor sports, there is sober advice to look to "mending laws, and . . . restoring trade" (118)—to remember his father's fate—to think of parliament as something more than "that house, where all our ills were shaped" (99)—and not to ignore the fact that the authority to make war (repeatedly mentioned) is what got his father into trouble.

Partially, this poem does give wise admonishment to the king; but it does so only partially, because Waller dared go no further, for he like half the kingdom was anxious about the extent of Charles's justice and mercy. At times in the poem we hear what might be expected from a cunning politician twice the king's age. Surveying the scene from the park, the king is imagined as observing Westminster, "Where royal heads receive the sacred gold:/ It gives them crowns, and does their ashes keep./ There made like gods, like mortals there they sleep" (92-94). The turn in the last line gives excellent point to the antithesis, there being little doubt which condition (reigning or being dead) is the more permanent. And in the middle of the poem, Waller devotes a tenth of his lines to a crucial if puzzling symbol. "Near this my Muse, what most delights her, sees/ A living gallery of aged trees;/ . . . With such old counselors they [kings] did advise,/ And, by frequenting sacred groves, grew wise" (67-73). Professor Miner relates this passage to emblematic literature, wherein the tree, especially the oak, carried overtones of royal authority and the old order.[30] But Waller has directed us to a *particular* association of these trees. They are "old counselors."

The overtones of royalty and tradition, like their age, reinforce this role. They point to the fairly young king's need for wise and experienced ministers. The king in fact followed this suggestion in the early years of his reign.

Finally, if its purpose was to persuade the king to continue his role as the reunifier and harmonizer of England, I would object against this poem that the poet's deifying of the king was counterproductive. His reign was marked by increasing sectarian conflict and regal stubbornness and arrogance. If, however, the purpose of the poem was merely to praise the king and to amuse him with the discovery of happy hieroglyphs in the park, one cannot object, but only fail to be as pleased as Charles, perhaps, was.

H.   "Instructions to a Painter"

In imaginative fabric, "Instructions to a Painter" is an excellent poem. Using the traditions of epic painting and epic poetry, Waller produces a well-made description and narration of the Duke of York's victory over the Dutch at Lowestoft in 1665. The dramatic device of the poet speaking to the painter enables the use of emblems and techniques of both arts, renders graphic the Wallerian understanding of the relationship of the poet to great deeds, and brings (to a much greater degree than usual in the political epigrams) the poet's sensibility into the poem. The poet, the enthusiastic observer, gives directions to the painter and shifts freely from one medium to the other:

> Painter! excuse me, if I have awhile
> Forgot thy art, and used another style;
> For, though you draw armed heroes as they sit,
> The task in battle does the Muses fit;
> They, in the dark confusion of a fight,
> Discover all, instruct us how to write;
> And light and honour to brave actions yield,
> Hid in the smoke and tumult of the field,
> Ages to come shall know that leader's toil,
> And his great name, on whom the Muses smile;
> Their dictates here let thy famed pencil trace,
> And this relation with thy colours grace. (287-98)

This notion of the superiority of poetry over painting, in depth of

perception, is perhaps derivative of Ben Jonson's poem on Lady
Venetia Digby, "Eupheme; or the Fair Fame Left to Posteritie,"
which in two of its sections employs the device of the poet's
directing, then dismissing, the painter;

> Painter yo' are come, but may be gone,
>
> . . .
> This worke I can performe alone;
>
> . . .
> You could make shift to paint an Eye,
>   An Eagle towring in the skye,
>   The Sunne, a Sea, or soundless Pit;
>   But these are like a Mind, not it.
> No, to expresse Mind to sense,
>   Would aske a Heavens Intelligence;
>   Since nothing can report that flame,
>   But what's of kinne to whence it came.

A further gain in the dramatic context is that Waller can,
especially at the beginning of the poem, use peremptory, striking
phrases with strong, imperative verbs (*draw, make, let, point*)
which have authoritative or epic overtones.

As narrative, the poem is organized around the central episode
of the death of "three worthy persons" standing next to the duke
during the battle. Preceding this episode, the scene is developed
carefully, on the canvas, and a brief encounter narrated whereby
the British take some merchantmen laden with wine (a proper
occasion for the poet to make some discoveries about Dutch
courage) and send the Dutch retreating to their own shores. The
retreat gives the duke opportunity, on the best epic models, to
combine love with valor:

> But who can always on the billows lie?
> The watery wilderness yields no supply.
> Spreading our sails, to Harwich we resort,
> And meet the beauties of the British court.
> The illustrious Duchess, and her glorious train,
> (Like Thetis with her nymphs) adorn the main. (77-82)

In the battle that follows the duke loses his three friends and
becomes an Achillean figure of rage and vengeance. He destroys
the Dutch admiral's ship and drives the fleet back toward

Holland. The imaginative structure of the poet-painter gives Waller's verse an even greater visual emphasis than usual, although he is preeminently a poet of the sense of sight and of plastic beauties: "burning ships the banished sun supply,/ And no light shines but that by which men die," (121-22) — "The flame invades the powder-rooms, and then,/ Their guns shoot bullets, and their vessels men./ The scorched Batavians on the billows float,/ Sent from their own, to pass in Charon's boat" (255-58). Although designed to evoke the scene at once in fact and on canvas, the description is wrought in the familiar Wallerian design of balance, paradox (death-bringing light), and turn, in the repetition of shooting (guns bullets, and ships men) and of boats (their own and then Charon's).

The poem concludes with instructions as to drawing the parliament and the king, the latter "high above them set," and the other "Pouring out treasure to supply his fleet" (300, 306). A Coda, "To the King," praises him extravagantly for developing the British navy:

> His club, Alcides, Phoebus has his bow,
> Jove has his thunder, and your navy you.
> . . .
>   Small were the worth of valour and of force,
> If your wisdom governed not their course;
> You as the soul, as the first mover you,
> Vigour and life on every part bestow;
> How to build ships, and dreadful ordnance cast,
> Instruct the artists, and reward their haste. (315-16, 323-28).

Irrelevant perhaps but irresistible is the presence of another artist in the scene; and although our awareness of circumstances beyond the poem includes him in the picture, he seems yet significant in the poem that concerns itself with actual events and relationships. I imagine Andrew Marvell overhearing the instructions that Waller gives to the painter. I imagine Marvell on many occasions, political as well as poetical, dogging Waller's steps. Although a careful study has not, to my knowledge, been made of parallels in poetic phrasing, there are many echoes of Waller in Marvell. And there are strong suggestions that Marvell learned something from Waller and very likely admired his felicitous touches as much as he disliked his politics and

temperament.[31]   It is, however, well established that Marvell
wrote a reply to the "Instructions"—a poem which, one might
say, established a genre, the painter poem. Also, Marvel had a
hand in one or more of several replies to it. Critics disagree as to
whether Marvell wrote "Second Advice to a Painter" or "Third
Advice," but "Last Instructions to a Painter" is generally
accounted his.[32] Having the facts and not having Waller's
purposes—apparently to rally support in the country and in the
parliament for the navy—Marvell capitalized on the Stuarts'
typical bad luck and their peculiar knack of achieving the
ruinous when the going was best; when the bad luck and the
peculiar knack are emphasized with heroic idiom and low detail,
they flip Waller's heroic mode into the mock heroic. The bad
luck and knack for the ruinous are well illustrated in David Ogg's
description of one episode in the battle of Lowestoft: "By 6 p.m.
the Dutch were in flight . . . when at 11 p.m. the duke turned in,
he left orders that the pursuit should be continued throughout
the night. There then occurred an accident typical of Stuart
history." The duke's fop secretary, thinking his master had
fought enough, ordered the captain to shorten sail. This being
done, the duke woke next morning in time "to see the enemy
escaping through the shallows into the Texel."[33]

In the parodic "The Last Instructions to a Painter," Marvell
moves the nonheroic facts into the foreground: the sorry state of
the navy, men not paid, docks falling down, jobbery in every
expenditure of funds. In an epic catalog of combatants in
parliamentary warfare, "Old Waller" is described as "Trumpet-
general," who "swore he'd write/ This Combat truer than the
navall Fight" (11.263-64).[34] The author of "The Second Advice
to a Painter" is even able to discover a good overlooked by
Waller (outdoing him in his own forte) in the death of a courtier
standing next to the duke: "Such was his rise, such was his fall,
unprais'd:/ A chance shot sooner took than chance him
rais'd./ His shatter'd head the fearless Duke disdains,/ And gave
the last-first proof that he had brains" (185-88).

Warren Chernaik has convincingly demonstrated Waller's role
in an historical development of heroic satire out of what I call
heroic epigram.[35] From Waller's poem on Charles I's escape at
sea to Alexander Pope's *To Augustus* there is a clear progression.
The strong aversion of Jonathan Swift and Pope to the flattery of
kings is symptomatic of the decline of regal panegyric (or its

"crisis"), which parallels the demythologizing of kingship in the seventeenth century. Two remarkable facts accentuate the decline: John Dryden's great pro-royal verse, achieved only by means of an amazing poetic ingenuity, and the dearth of great or significant poems of that kind after Dryden. If he praises a monster of a king, the poet himself creates ironies against his own intentions. As noted earlier, Cavalier amatory verse is graced with a play of ironic awareness, which, if present in Waller's Stuart panegyrics, would render them mock-heroic or, if controlled to suit his purpose, tend to raise them to the imaginative level of a masterpiece like Dryden's *Absalom and Achitophel.*

III *Courtesy and Myth*

Despite its Wallerian neatness of phrase, Alexander W. Allison's concession that Waller's poem are "aggregations of pleasantries"[36] does an injustice to the best qualities of the political epigrams, where often a pleasant manner disguises or expedites political savvy and rhetorical strategy. In a regal and aristocratic society, the courtesies must enfold the substance of communication, even if the system is collapsing, as can be seen in both Waller and a worthier poet, Ben Jonson. Jonson obviously speaks from a much better defended or stouter set of principles; his crustiness is a by-product of his integrity; yet he has a quality of urbanity such that his idealism is informed by a large experience in human life. Kingship after Jonson's time perhaps made the poet's task more difficult or even absurd, especially as the witty competition in outdoing compliments parallels less and less satisfactory models of royalty and an increasingly "modern" or secularized view of kingship.[37] Jonson seems able to maintain royalism without subservience:

> Who would not be thy subject, *James,* t'obay
> A Prince, that rules by' example, more than sway?
> Whose manners draw, more than thy powers constraine.
> And in this short time of thy happiest raigne,
> Hast purg'd thy realmes, as we have now no cause
> Left us of feare, but first our crimes, then lawes.
> (*Epigrammes,* XXXV, "To King James")

The reader senses a serious decline in Waller's praise of the grandson James: "His dreadful navy, and his lovely mind,/ Give him the fear and favour of mankind." The reader can give no credence at all to Waller's pleasure in "The growing greatness of our matchless King."[38]

Yet, Waller has a fine sense of the political realities and, when not completely thwarted by the roles assigned by fate to the Stuarts, weaves even his compliments into intricate, often wise, well-conceived and well-executed poetical wholes. They are often unsatisfactory poetic wholes, perhaps because readers anticipate Dryden's adding a dimension to such political verse, a dimension which one does find in Waller's songs. Nonetheless, Paul J. Korshin has found a measure of achievement in Waller's art: "What distinguishes Waller . . . is his attempts to establish a symbolic landscape of poetic forms in which certain analogies— typological, historical, classical—become standard referents."[39] And Earl Miner, as discussed earlier, has demonstrated the success of one such attempt in his analysis of "On St. James's Park." What is lacking, however, is the ironic mastery of the complex reality of the situation which one finds in the lyrics, because Waller was never able, in that sense, to conquer his political subjects. He set music for the powers of beauty to dance to, but was not quite able to do the same for political powers. In this respect Marvell, in his individualistic dissenting way, outdoes Waller and makes him appear weak and dishonest—except in some of Marvell's poems on Cromwell, where he becomes partisan and seems as mythopoeically exaggerated and inauthentic as Waller in his worst Stuart effusions. It is, finally, Dryden who brought to consummate form the art of using a "symbolic landscape" in political poetry. Dryden insinuates the mythic within a pattern and tone of sophisticated awareness. With Dryden, Charles II as David is never the two-dimensional monochrome of Waller's Charles II as Hercules or Charles I as Christ.

The danger poets ran in "Figural Interpretation" (the interpretation of a biblical event as prefiguring and thereby authorizing a latter-day event[40]) is that the event prefigured becomes a rationalistic or naturalistic explanation of the myth. Thus Waller as Phoebus in "The Story of Daphne and Phoebus, Applied" becomes an illustration of the etiology of such poetic "rages" as derangement in love. Cromwell prefigured as David implies as well an interpretation of David: do you mean, the reader asks the poet, that David was like what we see in

Cromwell? Or that St. James's Park, seen as another Eden, illustrates a fact-in-the-world—namely, dreams of paradise that will not last. Thomas Hobbes is the clearest participant in this way of understanding or vitiating myth (*Leviathan,* Chapter 45):

When our Saviour speaketh to the devil, and commandeth him to go out of a man, if by the devil he meant a disease, or frenzy, or lunacy, or a corporeal spirit, is not the speech improper? Can diseases hear? Or can there be a *corporeal* spirit in a body of flesh and bone, full already of vital and animal spirits? (Emphasis added.)

According to Hobbes, Christ utters a contradiction, which is not "improper" because the understanding of the audience was unenlightened and because the real meaning is in *signifying* the "power of God's word."

A mid-century poetic nexus of the trend is Sir William Davenant's *Gondibert,* the humanized or demythologized epic poem. Abraham Cowley praised Davenant in terms that reveal Cowley as poised between two modes of perception and discourse. After noting that supernatural beings appeared in earlier heroic poems, Cowley wrote:

> Thou like some worthy Knight, with sacred arms
> Dost drive the Monsters thence, and end the Charms.
> Instead of those dost Men and Manners plant,
> The things which that rich Soil did chiefly want.
> . . .
> So God-like Poets do past things reherse,
> Not change, but Heighten Nature by their Verse.[41]

The passage is charged with important poetic tendencies of the mid-century. Cowley speaks of *"sacred* arms" which are directed against formerly sacred things. Davenant becomes a Baconian hero (yet like a knight in a romance) who destroys medieval errors—a force for enlightenment, naturalism, science. But his achievement (presented in an image of starting anew— the idea at the heart of the modern and the progressivist) is figured in an application of the myth of Deucalion. In the last couplet, assuming a naturalistic mimetic theory of art, Cowley paradoxically limits godlike poets; they do not see beyond the surface of the "real," nor do they transform it, but rather merely heighten— decorate—it.

Waller's view is similar ("To Sir William Davenant, Upon His

First Two Books of *Gondibert"*). In *Gondibert,* Waller says,

> no bold tales of gods or monsters swell,
> But human passions, such as with us dwell.
> Man is thy theme; his virtue, or his rage,
> Drawn to the life in each elaborate page.
> . . .
> Such is thy happy skill, and such the odds
> Betwixt thy worthies and the Grecian gods!
> Whose deities in vain had here come down,
> Where mortal beauty wears the sovereign crown;
> Such as of flesh composed, by flesh and blood,
> Though not resisted, may be understood.

What is quietly advocated in the last four lines is the progressivist humanism of the Enlightenment. Zeus, in a myth we cannot now believe, once influenced human beings ("not resisted"). But now we have heroes who can be "understood." What is implicit is that the myths of the gods (unlike the gods in the myths) are now resisted and rejected in a naturalistic art. An anonymous writer gives an accurate representation of Waller's attitude toward myth in *Letters Supposed to Have Passed Between M. de St. Evremond and Mr Waller* (London, 1770), pp. 74-75: Waller is imagined as writing, "I often think, that the subaltern deities of the heathen bible were considered only as so many symboles of the universal parent." "Heathen bible" and "so many" are shrewd touches.

The myth emerging in the seventeenth century was that one could see the real as it is without myth. In Waller the force of mythic allusion is weakened both by a rational analysis of relationship to the real and by the clarity of the relationship. Usually there is one preeminent quality that governs the choice of an application—e.g., power is the important idea in the comparison of Charles II's navy to Hercules' club. What seems lost in this use of myth is that the allusion (the myth alluded to) is less "the case" than "about the case." In the eighteenth century a bishop in Waller's church was to say that the whole meaning of the communion service was a reminder to love one's neighbor— which is to say that celebration of the Eucharist is not an experience but about an experience.

Waller narrows myth on a rational line. In dense mythic verse, rightly admired and quoted, Waller refers to Amphion: "Those antique minstrels sure were Charles-like kings,/ Cities their lutes, and subjects' hearts their strings." It is the minstrels who are like Charles; Charles is the real example of the mythic generalization. That is to say, we now understand the myth of Amphion or Orpheus; they had Charles's power over the affections (or, more precisely, the power that he and the poet would like to imagine him having). The applications Waller uses, when in the least overdone, as is often the case, gives his verse an insincere or "skeptical" quality, the counterpart to the ironic detachment and play in the love poems, without a sense of wholeness of design. The discrepancy in Waller that David Hume noted (he is "as full of keen satyr and invective in his eloquence, as of tenderness and panegyric in his poetry") may be marked in the political poems: one suspects a satiric rictus behind the graceful smile.[42]

IV *The Navy and Peace*

From the beginning to the end of his poetic career, Waller wrote of the greatness of the British navy, even at times when that greatness was not so evident to others. In his earliest topic, Prince Charles's adventure at sea, he strikes the traditional note, so important in almost four hundred years of British self-interpretation, of dominion of the seas. Charles will become, the poet knows, "Lord of the scene where now his danger lies." As panegyrist of kings and a protector, Waller would naturally emphasize the navy as the most conspicuous part of their military power, which is connected in his mind with the constitutional power of the British king "of making War and Peace." Nearly every poem addressed to either Charles I, Cromwell, Charles II, or James II involves the notion of the ruler being "the sovereign of the sea." Even the poem on the reconstruction of St. Paul's manages to yoke the building of the church with that of the navy. St. Paul's itself is represented as in "the sea of time"; and Charles resembles Solomon, whose works "excelled/ His ships, and building." A major factor in Cromwell's claim to just rulership is his restoration of the navy's hegemony at sea: "Others may use the ocean as their road,/ Only the English make it their abode." The great power often occasions classical applications, as in the line addressed to Charles II: "Jove had his thunder, and your navy you."

The sea is perhaps a hieroglyph of a turning point in Waller's poetical career; in "At Penshurst" the poet, disappointed in love, is sent "to sea" by Apollo. Although much is obscure in his poems and life, at this point in the late 1630s, this may well mean that Waller leaves the amorous lyric for more serious themes, including the writing or reworking of poems that literally involve the sea: the poem about the king's escape at sea, "To the King on His Navy," "Of Salle," the ship of St. Paul's, a poem about his depression over the Sacharissa affair ("When He Was at Sea"), two poems addressed to the Lord Admiral (the Earl of Northumberland), and "The Battel of the Summer Islands," a mock-heroic so reminiscent of Edmund Spenser that one is tempted to find in it an obscured allegory.

For Waller to turn to the sea is to concern himself with more serious topics than ladies weaving or dancing or falling down in a path, or dwarfs marrying, or a girdle or the delicate complexities of courtship. It is to compose such a poem as "To the King on His Navy," which I assume was written some time after the imposition of and resistance to ship money in 1634. The theme of the poem is the security the British derive from a strong navy, which intimidates the French and Dutch into peace, makes the seas secure from piracy and warfare, and protects England from all "But winged troops, or Pegasean Horse." This strength is ennobled by a witty application from the Bible:

> Should nature's self invade the world again,
> And o'er the centre spread the liquid main,
> Thy power were safe, and her destructive hand
> Would but enlarge the bounds of thy command;
> Thy dreadful fleet would style thee lord of all,
> And ride in triumph o'er the drowned ball;
> Those towers of oak o'er fertile plains might go,
> And visit mountains where they once did grow,
> The world's restorer never could endure
> That finished Babel should those men secure,
> Whose pride designed that fabric to have stood
> Above the reach of any second flood;
> To thee, his chosen, more indulgent, he
> Dares trust such power with so much piety.

The outdoing image of British security in a second flood is turned neatly into a compliment to Charles, a fusion of piety and power, or as Thomas Rymer (the poem's greatest admirer) ecstatically noted, "Here is both *Homer* and *Virgil; the fortis Achilles* and the *pius Aeneas.*"[43] Samuel Johnson too was pleased with the lines on the flood, although he errs in thinking the word *centre* is misused: "those lines are very noble . . . so noble, that it were almost criminal to remark the mistake of centre for surface, or to say that the empire of the sea would be worth little if it were not that the waters terminate in land."[44]

Rymer insists on the value of the poem as art, separate from the reality of its claims: "The Thought and Application is most Natural, Just, and true in Poetry, tho' in fact, and really, He [Charles I] might have no more fortitude or piety, than another body."[45] In a poem about a concrete set of circumstances, such critical insistence actually calls the question into serious consideration. If we assume Waller was opposed in fact to ship money, as it was certainly in his interest to be, then this poem, if written during the years 1635–40, would seem inconsistent with his political behavior: his prosecuting of one of the ship-money judges and his alliance, at least for a while, with his cousin John Hampden. But Waller's view is not confined to his own interest, at least in the poems and in his parliamentary record. His sentiments are nearly always consonant with a reading of the role of England in European politics and with a somewhat idealized view of the English constitution. In 1675 he said in the House of Commons: "Let us look to our Government, Fleet, and Trade. 'Tis the advice that the oldest Parliament-man among you can give you." The fleet, vital to the military strength of the country in its role as peacemaker, is in the special care of the king (or the protector), who has the traditional or constitutional authority to wage war. Usually, it is true, Waller was consistent in asserting the Commons privilege of voting supply, inclined to go along with requests to a degree, while being thrifty with his and the people's money.

This is not to deny that this and other sea poems are lacking in aesthetic interest. It is clear that Waller was challenged poetically to represent seascapes. He works up gorgeous tableaus—especially in "Of the Danger His Majesty Escaped," "Of a War with Spain and a Fight at Sea," and "Instructions to a Painter"—tableaus of struggles in a small boat against a storm, of broadsides, of fires, of explosions.[46] Some of his most inventive images and witty rhetorical devices are inspired by the sea—for example, the image of England as a magic island in "A Panegyric to My Lord Protector":

> To dig for wealth we weary not our limbs;
> Gold, though the heaviest metal, hither swims;
> Ours is the harvest where the Indians mow;
> We plough the deep, and reap what others sow.

Waller's naval poems are both complimentary and admonitory. His real interest in the king's power is the peace it insures at sea and at home. The early emphasis in "To the King on His Navy" is that Charles has brought peace to the seas: "The French and Spaniard, when thy flags appear,/ Forget their hatred, and consent to fear." The same force, in "Of Salle," results in the clearing of the pirates who "scorned all power and laws of men." Precisely the same claim—that military strength creates peace for England and often for Europe—is made for Cromwell, Charles II, and James II. Before the Civil War, Waller seems to have viewed naval aggressive potential more narrowly as a means of venting internal tensions:

> Heaven sends, quoth I, this discord for our good,
> To warm, perhaps, but not to waste our blood;
> To raise our drooping spirits, grown the scorn
> Of our proud neighbors, who ere long shall mourn
> (Though now they joy in our expected harms)
> We had occasion to resume our arms.

The idea is repeated in praise of Cromwell, who "Found nobler objects for our martial rage"—that is, the Dutch and the Spanish rather than "ourselves," the Scots, or the Irish—"And, with wise conduct, to his country showed/ The ancient way of conquering abroad./ . . . [he] gave us peace and empire too."[47]

In respect of such a view of war, as in other ways, Fairfax's translation of Tasso's *Godfrey of Bullogne* seems to have been an early and unending influence on Waller. Dryden noted the indebtedness to Fairfax: "many besides myself have heard our famous Waller own, that he derived the harmony of his numbers from *Godfrey of Bulloign*, which was turned into English by Mr. Fairfax."[48] Aside from metrical harmony Waller also learned a pan-Christian bias against the infidel, which broadened his irenic vision of England generously into a Europe harmonized against the "Turk." In a poem "To His Worthy Friend, Sir Thos. Higgons," Waller complained of Europeans who

> Shed Christian blood, and populous cities raze,
> Because they're taught to use some different phrase.
> If, listening to your charms, we could our jars
> Compose, and on the Turk discharge these wars,
> Our British arms the sacred tomb might wrest
> From Pagan hands, and triumph o'er the East;
> And then you might our own high deeds recite,
> And with great Tasso celebrate the fight.

Although first printed in 1658, this poem was first published in Waller's collected works in 1682, when intra-Christian hostility was maddening round the land; and the same theme appears in a poem addressed to the Catholic James II, with hopes for avoidance of sectarian fighting by venting hostility in a new crusade:

> The Turk's vast empire does united stand;
> Christians, divided under the command
> Of jarring princes, would be soon undone,
> Did not this hero make their interest one;
> Peace to embrace, ruin the common foe,
> Exalt the Cross, and lay the Crescent low.

Lest Waller's strategies for peace at home appear simply patriotic, it should be noted that his natural (perhaps pusillanimous) desire to avoid conflict found larger concentric circles of expression.[49] Of James II's intercession to bring about an accommodation among several belligerent nations in 1686, Waller wrote: "So Peaceful! and so valiant! are extremes,/ Not to be found, but in our matchless James./ . . . Your nobler art of making peace destroys/ The barbarous foe, without expense or noise." And finally, in his last major poetic enterprise, *Of Divine Love*, Waller makes his own truce with the Turks, speaking of Christ:

> Love as he loved! A love so unconfined,
> With arms extended, would embrace mankind.
> Self-love would cease, or be dilated, when
> We should behold as many selfs as men;
> All of our family, in blood allied,
> His precious blood, that for our ransom died.

This progression from an enthusiasm for "monarchs of the sea" to an advocacy of universal charity and peace is perhaps of little interest in itself. Yet in this, and in other ways, Waller anticipates both the principles of many important persons and the historical events of the English nation in the century that was to follow his own: Jonathan Swift defending the Peace of Utrecht, Alexander Pope affirming benevolence in *An Essay on Man*, politicians as diverse as Robert Harley and Robert Walpole devoting themselves to ending or avoiding war, England itself after 1714 enjoying an era of relatively minor international conflict. The fact that Waller's reputation maintained an impressive height from the Restoration to at least the 1760s is probably due to his responding to political and poetical developments in a way that struck those who followed him as normal and inevitable.

CHAPTER 4

Waller's View of Art and His Place in English Literature

I   Waller's View of Art

A.   The Orphic Forces

L ITTLE attention need to be paid to the commendatory verses which good nature prompted him [Waller] to address to such of his friends as were authors," wrote G. Thorn-Drury in his brief commentary on the poetry.[1] For several reasons I believe the judgment to be wrong. Waller wrote a number of poems to and about artists: "To Mr. Henry Lawes," "To Mr. George Sandys," "To Vandyck," "Upon Ben Jonson," "To Sir William Davenant," "To His Worthy Friend, Master Evelyn," "Upon the Earl of Roscommon's Translation of Horace." Reflections upon art are a persistent theme in diverse poems throughout his career; and, as I shall try to show in the second part of this chapter, his poems to artists and about art elucidate his position in English literature.

Still another reason may be adduced as refutation of Thorn-Drury's dismissal of the poems to authors (and, as the topic naturally broadens, about art). Waller is essentially a poet of powers. Either every subject is a potent agency, or he discovers potency in it—whether a beautiful woman, a king, the British navy, a work of art, God. Their virtue (or power) is their capacity to affect, to move. Poetry, rhetoric, all arts, thus regarded in terms of their impact, naturally appear analogous to persons who *amaze* by means of some characteristic—beauty, nobility, power. A poem about such a person is a curious replication of his effect in the real world. Art imitates nature in its effects, which are most analogous to the effects of art.

Orpheus and Amphion are the mythic *loci* of the "powers" — the power of art, artists, ladies, political leaders.[2]   Waller's interest in their myths is almost exclusively *in what with music they effected*,[3] just as audience impact is his major concern in art. In most of his poems he directly or indirectly teases with ideas of the relationships among diverse powers of art and nature. Consider a poem that is perfectly representative and that was probably written about the time of the "Panegyric" on Cromwell:

> ### Of a Tree Cut in Paper
> Fair hand! that can on virgin paper write,
> Yet from the stain of ink preserve it white;
> Whose travel o'er that silver field does show
> Like track of leverets in morning snow.
> Love's image thus in purest minds is wrought,
> Without a spot or blemish to the thought.
> Strange that your fingers should the pencil foil,
> Without the help of colours or of oil!
> For though a painter boughs and leaves can make,
> 'Tis you alone can make them bend and shake;
> Whose breath salutes your new-created grove,
> Like southern winds, and makes it gently move.
> Orpheus could make the forest dance; but you
> Can make the motion and the forest too.
> A poet's fancy when he paints a wood,
> By his own nation only understood,
> Is as in language so in fame confined;
> Not like to yours, acknowledged by mankind.
> All that know Nature and the trees that grow,
> Must praise the foliage expressed by you,
> Whose hand is read wherever there are men:
> So far the scissor goes beyond the pen.

The poem charms in spite of its almost absurd compliment; indeed the challenge to the poet is to present that lady's art form as, paradoxically, the ultimate one. Waller's ingenuity, the *poet's* fine scissors work, is to discover argument, application, image which prove the superiority of her *metier*. First is the innocence that nevertheless creates; paper is wrought, without stain, into art, with the implication of superiority to literature, which involves a stain on the virgin sheet. The image of leverets in the snow identifies her art with the agency of nature, while the next couplet (comparing her art to chaste ideas of love) makes a connection with transcending Platonic forms, beyond nature. The rest of the poem (7–22) consists of more direct comparisons to other kinds of artists. The central device is a chiasmus or double turn (Puttenham's *antimetabole)* on the idea *make-image* and *move-image.* The superiority to written art (established earlier in the poem) is extended to painting, which the lady-artist outdoes by being able not only to *make* trees but also to *move* them (by blowing or shaking). Orpheus could *move* but not *make* trees. Last, the lady's art exceeds the poet's for hers is a universal language, understood by "All that know Nature and the trees that grow."

Of course it is Waller the poet whose art discovers or creates such all-powerful significance in the lady's craft. In such a poem, as in "lapidary inscriptions" (to borrow Johnson's authority), "a man is not upon oath." The subject is slight, the tone gallant, but ironic. The poet's devices imply a thorough subjectivity and intellectual sleight-of-hand. The reader, the poet, and the lady know that the magnification is specious, but the awareness does not undercut the lady's, nor the poet's, serious intention and capability to delight with dainty craft. Also, if the images are reversed—Orpheus, poets, painters are *like* this slight artist—the irony turns full circle to the ultimate triviality and ephemerality of all art.

Confirmation of the presence of this theme exists in a sequel to the poem, the title of which explains the connection:

To a Lady,
From Whom He Received the Foregoing Copy
Which for Many Years Had Been Lost.

Nothing lies hid from radiant eyes;
All they subdue become their spies.
Secrets, as choicest jewels, are
Presented to oblige the fair;
No wonder, then, that a lost thought
Should there be found, where souls are caught.
   The picture of fair Venus (that
For which men say the goddess sat)
Was lost, till Lely from your look

> Again that glorious image took.
>   If Virtue's self were lost, we might
> From your fair mind new copies write.
> All things but one you can restore;
> The heart you get returns no more.

The lady's power now is the power to preserve art. The poet's lost poem is imagined as held in ideal form, by the lady: "No wonder, then, that a lost thought/ Should there be found, where souls are caught." A central image again relates the arts and nature: the painter Lely remakes the image of Venus from her. Thus she has served art in recapturing beauty—the beauty of the previous poem (a rather outdoing compliment of the poet to himself!); and she has the potentiality of furnishing, to art, ideas or forms of virtue, should they be lost. Last, the poet calls the reader's attention to the power of the lady's attractiveness, which is neatly presented as an antithetic limit on her powers of restoration.

The orphic understanding of art pervades Waller's poetry, early and late, especially (as noted earlier) the Sacharissa poems. "On My Lady Dorothy Sidney's Picture" gives the effect of looking at an object reflected through a series of opposed mirrors. The speaker discovers in the picture that Dorothy excels the representation of beauty in two heroines created by her famous great-uncle, Sir Philip Sidney. In his *Arcadia*, the pictures alone of the heroines, Philocla and Pamela, had been sufficient to inspire Pyrocles and Musidorus to love. In Waller's poem, Dorothy's picture (art) has the same effect on him, with the complimentary difference that her image embodies in *one* the beauty her kinsman could not reduce to fewer than *two* forms. In "fact" the niece accomplishes what art could not: "Just nature, first instructed by his thought,/ In his own house thus practised what he taught;/ This glorious piece transcends what he could think,/ So much his blood is nobler than his ink!" Dorothy is a refutation of Sidney's aesthetic idealism: the brazen world exceeds the golden. Or, at any rate, the lady is so to understand. But her beauty is here (in the poem) *represented;* the poet invents the outdoing analogies, he uses the resources of Sidney's art in his own, so that, ironically, Sidney's aesthetic triumphs, after all, as the golden beauty of Dorothy is realized by the painting and in the poem.

"To Vandyck" seems to undercut the power of art, the lady more beautiful than her portrait.

> Yet who can tax thy [Vandyck's] blameless skill,
> Though thy good hand had failed still,
> When nature's self so often errs?
> She for this many thousand years
> Seems to have practised with much care,
> To frame the race of women fair;
> Yet never could a perfect birth
> Produce before to grace the earth,
> Which waxed old ere it could see
> Her that amazed thy art and thee.

The poet has found a cosmic solution to an apparent problem; the painter had needed several sittings—more than usual—for the portrait. In this, as revealed in the lines just quoted, he can be seen (honorifically) as simply imitating nature, which has struggled so long to bring forth such beauty. Also, gallantly, the speaker suggests the painter wanted more sittings in order to enjoy the lady's beauty—and thus by such craft to lose the reputation of mastery of his art: "Confess, and we'll forgive thee this;/ For who would not repeat that bliss?/ And frequent sight of such a dame/ Buy with the hazard of his fame?" The poem begins and ends with emphasis on the power of art:

> Rare Artisan, whose pencil moves
> Not our delights alone, but loves!
> . . .
> O let me know
> Where those immortal colours grow,
> That could this deathless piece compose!
> In lilies? or the fading rose?
> No; for this theft thou has climbed higher
> Than did Prometheus for his fire.

Again, slyly, in the images of the lilies and the *fading* rose, the poet insinuates a superiority of art, just as earlier he has for his own persuasive designs suggested an advantage in the painting— the lady is kinder there: "Fool! that forgets her stubborn look/ This softness from thy [the painter's] finger took." The application of Prometheus suggests, too, the greater power of artistry, while complimenting the lady. The painter had done the amazing deed, heroically finding the means to recreate the lady's beauty in more permanent form.

The first of two poems entitled "At Penshurst" (beginning "Had Sacharissa lived . . ."), attributes to the lady all the poetical powers of Orpheus and Amphion; her beauty, like art, is civilizing and harmonizing. She is a true niece of Sir Philip, on whose tree the humble poet carves his passion; and she is of such orphic worth that the speaker dares do no more than admire. The theme of the poem is a turn: a poet's niece and a poet's love have the virtues (powers) of the greatest poets. As noted earlier, these virtues Waller returns to himself in "The Story of Phoebus and Daphne, Applied," for the lady's rejection causes him to reach an Apollonian fame: "All, but the nymph that should redress his wrong,/ Attend his passion, and approve his song."

In the second "At Penshurst" the orphic attributes transfer to the poet, whose power of song moves everything but the lady, who (with such poetic ancestry) should know how to respond. Nature hearkens now, not to her, but to him: "While in the park I sing, the listening deer/ Attend my passion, and forget to fear./ When to the beeches I report my flame,/ They bow their heads, as if they felt the same." He skillfully applies orphic power to the conventions of the courtly situation: he hurts himself with his complaint:

> Thy heart no ruder than the rugged stone,
> I might, like Orpheus, with my numerous moan
> Melt to compassion; now, my traitorous song
> With thee conspires to do the singer wrong;
> While thus I suffer not myself to lose
> The memory of what augments my woes;
> But with my own breath still foment the fire,
> With flames as high as fancy can aspire!

The Sacharissa poems begin with the poet's accepting a challenge—to win a beautiful woman by the power of verse (by means of poetic beauty). The poetic context of the courtship affords many occasions for complex oppositions and turns on art and reality. A kind of competition between the beauty of woman versus the beauty of art proceeds first in the poet's ironic suggestion of the superiority of his craft, then to the poet's assumption of the powers, and concludes in a (temporary?) renunciation of poetry when its power becomes self-destructive, as Apollo counsels Waller to hang up his lute. Considered as a sequence of poems on a sustained theme, the Sacharissa poems are an account of the poet's falling in love with his craft.

B.   Mimetic Art, Platonic Forms, and the Golden World of Poetry

Waller very likely wrote his tribute to Jonson ("Upon Ben Jonson," first published in *Jonsonus Virbius* in 1638) during his courtship of Sacharissa. It is a witty compliment derived from the mimetic theory of art; a central zeugma ("Whoever in those glasses looks, may find/ The spots returned, or graces, of his mind") unifies a fairly complex scheme of techniques including the familiar Wallerian turn, paradox, application. There is a slight parodic effect of Jonson's style, along with an impression that the poem is a bit "got up." The theme is that Jonson is master of the greatest mimetic art — an art with the power to imitate the real world (of diverse experience) and the ideal world (of absolute value, in the forms of the mind). And in the *real* world Jonson has become the *ideal* poet:

> Mirror of poets! mirror of our age!
> . . .
> Thou hast alone those various inclinations
> Which Nature gives to ages, sexes, nations,
> So traced with thy all-resembling pen,
> That whate'er custom has imposed on men,
> . . .
> Is represented to the wondering eyes
> Of all that see, or read, thy comedies.
> Whoever in those glasses looks, may find
> The spots returned, or graces, of his mind;
> And by the help of so divine an art,
> At leisure view, and dress, his nobler part.
> Narcissus, cozened by that flattering well,
> Which nothing could but of his beauty tell,
> Had here, discovering the deformed estate
> Of his fond mind, preserved himself with hate.
> But virtue too, as well as vice, is clad
> In flesh and blood so well, that Plato had
> Beheld, what his high fancy once embraced,
> Virtue with colours, speech, and motion graced.

As in the Sacharissa poems, the distinctions between art and nature work toward compliment and persuasion (the strategy of the poem is to bring us to accept the praise of Jonson). Jonson's poetry becomes a solution to the old challenge to art, from the philosopher Plato, that it was but an imitation of an imitation. Jonson has mastered both the ephemeral world of convention and the eternal world of ideal forms and absolute truth; and, in his teaching craft, the ideal is made to enter into the real world, as the neat application of Narcissus reveals. Besides being a social historian without equal, Jonson also achieves Sir Philip Sidney's standards of the poet-idealists, who "most properly do imitate to teach & delight: and . . . range onely reined with learned discretion, into the divine consideration of what may be and should be. . . . For these indeed do meerly make to imitate, and imitate both to delight & teach, and delight to move men to take that goodnesse in hand, which without delight they would flie as from a stranger; and teach to make them know that goodnesse wherunto they are moved."[4] While the play on ideas of form and mirrors, variety and unity, the conventional versus the ideal, maintains a serious motion of compliment (which has a Jonsonian effect of more verve and spring than a customary Wallerian smoothness) — Waller adds a touch of Jonsonian independence and humor, reminiscent of Carew's crusty Jonsonian rebuke of Jonson in "To Ben Jonson, Upon Occasion of His Ode of Defiance Annex'd to His Play of 'The New Inn.' "[5] Waller's tribute works by discovery of claims of the all-encompassing power of Jonson's art; and of Jonson himself, the assertion is,

> [thy] fate's no less peculiar than thy art;
> For as thou couldst all characters impart,
> So none could render thine, which still escapes,
> Like Proteus, in variety of shapes;
> Who was nor this, nor that, but all we find,
> And all we can imagine, in mankind.

Thus his personality is the mirror of his art: various in occupation, achievement, mood. Perhaps more rhetorical than convincing is the parallel of his having all real *and* imaginary qualities. But Jonsonian in spirit are the directness about his variety of enterprises (does the reader correctly think of bricklaying?) and the pun on the man's size. The poem is a contrivance which keeps on us a rhetorical torsion but ends with an impression that the voice we've heard is wry, ironic, truthful. Waller is here more Jonsonian than usual, except perhaps in the great lyrics.

"To Mr. Henry Lawes, Who Had Then Newly Set a Song of Mine in the Year 1635," like many of Waller's poems, brings to mind more famous Augustan aftereffects. The theme is the familiar power of music, appropriately figured in the musically related device of a turn: "Verse makes heroic virtue *live;*/ But you can *life* to verses give." The secondary themes of the poem reveal a spirit of rational clarity championed by Malherbe in France and a reconciliation of the Ramist division of dialectic and rhetoric (or the opposition between sense and decoration):[6]

> As a church window, thick with paint,
> Lets in a light but dim and faint;
> So others, with division [a "florid melodic passage"] hide
> The light of sense, the poet's pride:
> But you alone may truly boast
> That not a syllable is lost;
> The writer's, and the setter's skill
> At once the ravished ears do fill.
> Let those which only warble long,
> And gargle in their throats a song,
> Content themselves with Ut, Re, Mi:
> Let words, and sense, be set by thee.

The ideals expressed here, if not realized in the verse itself, nonetheless became the highest values in the achievement of Alexander Pope: the vitalization of heroic virtue, the fusion of rhetorical technique and moral sense, and a forceful clarity of expression.

As noted earlier, Waller seems to have been especially sensitive to visual or plastic beauty, which he often figures in images of light. The power of the beauty of women is analogous in his mind to that of art; and a number of his poems are about their mutual reinforcement. A nearly perfect statement in miniature of his aesthetics is "On My Lady Isabella, Playing on the Lute," its theme being the familiar power of beauty (of woman and song) to move. The lady's style is itself Wallerian:

> Such moving sounds from such a careless touch!
> So unconcerned herself, and we so much!

What art is this, that with so little pains
Transports us thus, and o'er our spirit reigns?

Typically in Waller's wit, after an antithesis or juxtaposition establishes itself, he works a new twist or reversal out of the ordinary sense of the relationship. Thus, from the equation woman's beauty=beauty in art, he works a number of variations mainly on the topic of the power of both. However, in the poems solely about woman's beauty, the interest has often been the enjoyment of the beauty before it fades. What if this topic is placed back into the equation, if *fading* is related to art? The result is "Of English Verse," where the sadness of the death of beauty attaches to art itself. It is a sobering thought (though not one expressed in so many words in this poem) that, eventually on this planet, even Shakespeare's plays will come to dust. The evidence of the loss of art is found in the English language, which was perceived by Waller and his contemporaries as impermanent: "Poets that lasting marble seek,/ Must carve in Latin, or in Greek,/ We write in sand, our language grows,/ And, like the tide, our work o'erflows." There is an irony in the alleged permanence of Greek and Latin inscriptions, for the older the inscribing, the greater the decay. Is the apparent mixing of metaphors unfelicitous—the conventional *writing in sand* (with what?) being obliterated by *rising water* (the growing language)? Perhaps it succeeds against the sense. It is Chaucer who illustrates the point of decay: "the glory of his numbers lost," a reference to the Renaissance-neoclassical misunderstanding, which Waller shares, of Chaucer's syllabification.

But this circumstance, the loss of art, is not the final one, as the poet surprises the reader by asserting a quaint compensation for art. "And yet he [Chaucer] did not sing in vain," *because* the ladies "Rewarded with success his love." Returning to the equation, it appears that the decay of art may be used again to suggest that beauty should be enjoyed without delay. But not quite—the ladies rewarded the poet because he promised them immortality. That is to say, they were deceived; for, as the first half of the poem establishes, English verse itself will waste and die:

This was the generous poet's scope;
And all an English pen can hope,

> To make the fair approve his flame,
> That can *so far* extend their fame.
>
> Verse, thus designed, has no ill fate,
> If it arrive but at the date
> Of fading beauty; if it prove
> But as long-lived as present love.

The two words "so far," emphasized above, add ambiguity. Do they mean *as long as Chaucer's poems have lasted?* Or, as the last stanza elaborates, only *as long as woman's beauty or a love affair lasts?* It is possible that the real strategy of the poem is in the *carpe diem* mode (and is similar to Robert Herrick's "Corinna") with a deliberate collapsing of the fates of the poet-speaker and the lady as persuasion toward a further sharing, in the enjoyment of present beauty and present love.

"Of English Verse" is atypical of Waller's poems in which a perception of the golden or good in events and persons usually prevails. The selectivity of his topics itself establishes a pattern as he chooses subjects naturally honorific in themselves: love, heroic action, the creation of beauty. A delightful product of his Pollyanna muse is "To Zelinda," a poem which recalls the situation with Sacharissa, for Zelinda (a character in a romance by Des Marets) "Expresses her determination to wed none but a Prince."[7] Imagining himself as the suitor of the ambitious lady, Waller presents to her arguments for natural as opposed to conventional aristocracy; this argument includes one admirably economical line: " 'Tis not from whom, but where, we live." He then uses the traditional arguments that poets perceive and preserve in golden form the fame of the greatest human beings — just as he is prepared to do for her:

> Smile but on me, and you shall scorn,
> Henceforth, to be of princes born.
> I can describe the shady grove
> Where your loved mother slept with Jove;
> And yet excuse the faultless dame,
> Caught with her spouse's shape and name.
> Thy matchless form will credit bring
> To all the wonders I shall sing.

As in his *carpe diem* poems generally, here — in a poem about a

woman in a romance — Waller makes me believe in a real woman
he is using all his craft to seduce. The most convincing detail is
the last couplet, which (after assertion of the poet's power
through much of the poem) courteously concedes the greater
power of her beauty and, of course, presents a compliment likely
to charm a real woman like Zelinda. However, if the woman was
Dorothy Sidney, then it did not work, or at any rate did not lead
to matrimony.

C.   Didacticism and Propriety

"Upon the Earl of Roscommon's Translation of Horace" is the
fullest expression of Waller's poetic creed and is, like the poem
to Lawes, at once a harbinger of English Augustanism and a
recovery of values from largely classical and neoclassical
sources: Roman poetic theory itself in the Horatian expression,
the rationalism and self-control (with yet a dash of the Cavalier)
typical of Falkland's Great Tew circle, the emphasis on clarity
and order, the distrust of inspiration advocated by a generation
of French poets after Malherbe,[8] and the principles and practice
of the English poets Sidney and Jonson. Like the longer and
greater work which it perhaps influenced, Pope's *Essay on
Criticism*, the poem is open to the censure that it is merely a
collection of truisms. They are, however, truisms that were
passionately held to be true; and they are doctrines of art that
Waller followed closely in most of his poems. The one major
poetic activity that does not fit into the scheme of values of the
poem to Roscommon is the composition of love lyrics. In an
earlier poem to Davenant, Waller assigned to the poet the task of
teaching "present youth" how to love. The omission is a
prefiguring of the neoclassic seriousness — stooping to truth and
moralizing the song.

That the translation of Horace was made by an earl is a
reminder of an important phenomenon associated with a
gentleman-poet (or nobleman-poet): an aversion to impressions
of hard work or odors of the lamp. Waller knows to praise
Roscommon for avoiding such an impression, just as his own
poems reveal a commitment to what is perhaps very nearly
identical with Cavalier *insouciance* or *sprezzatura* — the effect,
as has been wittily observed, of having composed verses while
falling off a horse. Waller hails Roscommon as "Britain! whose

genius is in verse expressed,/ Bold and sublime, but negligently dressed." The poem divides, both in its topics and in formal organization, into (a) considerations of the standards of poetry and (b) expression of the social functions or purposes of poetry.

The major worth claimed for Roscommon's translation of *The Art of Poetry* is that it teaches poets important truths about their craft. The "rules" of writing become clear. One must exercise self-control: "Direct us how to back the winged horse,/ Favour his flight, and moderate his force." Inspiration is destructive without moderation and discipline: the opposition of wit to judgment to which Hobbes gave forceful expression and currency is echoed in: "He that proportioned wonders can disclose,/ At once his fancy and his judgment shows." Characteristically, Waller is able to discover a virtue in a less worthy by-product of poetic judgment—the words and lines that the poet *rejects:* "Poets lose half the praise they should have got,/ Could it be known what they discreetly blot."

He insists unequivocally on the importance of the ethical didactic: "Chaste moral writing we may learn from hence, / Neglect of which no wit can recompense./ . . . Well-sounding verses are the charm we use,/ Heroic thoughts and virtue to infuse." Illustrating the strategy that Dryden and others thought Waller had brought to English verse, Waller asserts the preeminence of management of "sound":

> Well-sounding verses are the charm we use,
> Heroic thoughts and virtue to infuse;
> Things of deep sense we may in prose unfold,
> But they move more in lofty numbers told.
> By the loud trumpet, which our courage aids,
> We learn that sound, as well as sense, persuades.

A principle more peculiarly his is Waller's denigration of satiric verse (an oddity in a poem about a translation of Horace):

> The fountain which from Helicon proceeds,
> That sacred stream! should never water weeds,
> Nor make the crop of thorns and thistles grow,
> Which envy or perverted nature sow.
>
> . . .
>
> The Muses' friend, unto himself severe,
> With silent pity looks on all that err.

The social, political, moral purpose of poetry is implicit in the insistence on "chaste moral" content. The purposes further stated are similarly Roman and poignantly utopian, considered in context of the politics of 1680, the date of publication of Waller's poem. Great public achievements, political as well as military, the poet rewards "with his immortal lines." And though less explicitly stated, more impressively set forth in images, is the power of poets' words to bring unity and harmony to a state:

> Such [words] as, of old, wise bards employed to make
> Unpolished men their wild retreats forsake;
> Law-giving heroes, famed for taming brutes,
> And raising cities with their charming lutes;
> For rudest minds with harmony were caught,
> And civil life was by the Muses taught.
> So wandering bees would perish in the air,
> Did not a sound, proportioned to their ear,
> Appease their rage, invite them to the hive,
> Unite their force, and teach them how to thrive,
> To rob the flowers, and to forbear the spoil,
> Preserved in winter by their summer's toil;
> They give us food, which may with nectar vie,
> And wax, that does the absent sun supply.

If these lines are read as apology for the panegyrics and political epigrams, and if compared in spirit with Waller's Plot and his parliamentary career, the worthiness of at least the highest intentions can be claimed for the man and his work. The poem contains a unified vision of the poetic and the political, as demonstrated in the movement from the beginning of the poem with its concern for control of poetic "rage" to the conclusion where the poet aims at appeasing public "rage." Oddly enough, while what Waller intended in his political actions and in his poems emerged in "the peace of the Augustans" after the Glorious Revolution (which he did not live to see), the reduction of "rage" in political life came about in spite of the Stuarts and in spite of Wallerian orphic sounds for harmonious royalism.

In nearly all respects during his last years Waller was a model of propriety. He was generally sober in an age of heavy drinking. In his parliamentary career, after the Restoration, he exhibited exemplary behavior. It is as if in his life, as in his verse, the pleasant, the good were to be magnified: thus the development out of the Lydian mode of his love poems to the Horatian idealism of the poem on Roscommon; thus the advocacy of the neoclassical didactic, as Knightly Chetwood recorded in "The Life of Virgil" prefixed to Dryden's translation. Chetwood takes note of Vergil's doctrine that poetry should inculcate virtue and adds that this "was the Principle too of our Excellent Mr. *Waller,* who us'd to say that he wou'd raze any Line out of his Poems, which did not imply some Motive to Virtue."[9] Thorn-Drury's Victorian comment is that if Waller's poems "are not didactic throughout, this at least should be remembered in his favour, that he lived through the period of the Restoration without suffering anything he wrote to be disfigured by the slightest trace of obscenity."[10]

Of course, the exemplary way of growing old is to become proper, didactic, pious, and "sage." One of Waller's last poems, "Of the Last Verses in the Book," and perhaps his most memorable image, discovers the goods in growing old, the power or virtue in dying:

> The soul's dark cottage, battered and decayed,
> Lets in new light through chinks that time has made;
> Stronger by weakness, wiser men become,
> As they draw near to their eternal home.
> Leaving the old, both worlds at once they view,
> That stand upon the threshold of the new.

And, fittingly, his last large poetic undertaking was *Divine Poems,* made up primarily of three of his longer (but hardly his better) poems: "Of Divine Love," "Of Divine Poesy," and "On the Fear of God." In the last of the three he brings to proper close his long life and poetical career, penitent and hopeful and, in his customary way, seeing the happy side:

> Wrestling with death, these lines I did indite;
> No other theme could give my soul delight.
> O that my youth had thus employed my pen!
> Or that I now could write as well as then!
> But 'tis of grace, if sickness, age, and pain,
> Are felt as throes, when we are born again;
> Timely they come to wean us from this earth,
> As pangs that wait upon a second birth.

As the spirit of Stuart restoration wore itself and the kingdom out, Waller, like Dryden, began to see his age in a starker light: he declaimed against "This Iron Age (so fraudulent and bold!)" — and, most significantly, applications to Moses and Deborah replace those of Orpheus and Amphion. Waller tried at the end to recapture for poetry what perhaps he had helped to lose, or what in his *application* of myth had been slipping away. His was the countercurrent to the mythopoesis of a bard like Milton. Thus, it is in the failure rather than in the example of his *Divine Poems* that we see the force of John Dennis's observation (*The Grounds of Criticism in Poetry,* 1704): "I have reason to believe, that one of the principal Reasons that has made the modern Poetry so contemptible, is, that by divesting it self of Religion, it is fallen from its Dignity, and its original Nature and Excellence; and from the greatest Production of the Mind of Man, is dwindled to an extravagant and a vain Amusement."[11]

II   *Waller's Place in English Literature*

A.   Waller's "Smoothness"

If one accepts the validity of John Aubrey's account, Waller established a poetic goal for himself with a specific attitude toward the English tradition: "[Waller was] one of our first refiners of our English language and poetry. When he was a brisque young sparke, and first studyed Poetry; me thought, sayd he, I never sawe a good copie of English verses; *they want smoothness;* then I began to essay."[12]

Perhaps one may provisionally separate the fact of Waller's melodiousness from the "achievement" suggested in Aubrey's account and insisted on by a number of contemporaries, until it became what René Welek has called the *fable convenue* of the Augustans[13]—that the language was crude and the verse harsh until refinement and melody were inaugurated by Waller and brought to perfection by Dryden and Pope.

Setting aside the *fable* for a moment, I wish to note that there is little basis to doubt Waller's melodiousness, which is apparent to any reader of the songs and lyrical epigrams. It is another matter, however, to assert that he invented it. The earliest critical comments on Waller include, and very nearly consist entirely of, praise of his smoothness. Clement Barksdale

(Nympha Liberthris, or the Cotswold Muse—London, 1651)
wrote that "Your [Waller's] Name shall be enrolled Sir, among/
Best English Poets, who write *smooth and strong."* On a number
of occasions, over a period of thirty years, John Dryden made a
similar claim. In 1664 ("Epistle Dedicatory" to *The Rival
Ladies),* he observed that the "sweetness of Mr. Waller's lyric
poesy was afterwards followed in the epic by Sir John Denham."
In 1668 ("An Essay of Dramatic Poesy"), he has a character in a
dialogue assert that "nothing [is] so even, sweet, and flowing, as
Mr. Waller." In 1672 ("Defence of the Epilogue"), Dryden
attributed to Waller an almost incredible role in English
literature: "Well-placing of words, for the sweetness of pronun-
ciation, was not known till Mr. Waller introduced it." And in 1693
("A Discourse Concerning the Original and Progress of Satire"),
he put on record a judgment that few can share today: Spenser's
verse is "so numerous, so various, and so harmonious" that he is
"surpassed" only by Vergil and Waller.[14] Nor does Edward
Phillips, Milton's pupil and nephew, differ on this point from
Barksdale and Dryden *(Theatrum Poetarum*—London, 1675):
"Edmund Waller . . . one of the most fam'd Poets, and that not
unworthy. . . . especially, and (wherein he is not inferiour to
Carew himself,) in the charming sweetness of his Lyric Odes or
amorous Sonnets. . . . In his other occasional Poems his Verse is
Smooth, yet strenuous."

The writers just quoted, the panegyrists of *Poems to the
Memory of that Incomparable Poet Edmond Waller Esquire*
(including Sir Thomas Higgons, Thomas Rymer, St. Evremond,
Aphra Behn), Addison, Pope, Elijah Fenton, Goldsmith, Johnson,
and many other seventeenth and eighteenth century critics
agree Waller's verse was "sweet." Pope's expression is the most
famous: "praise the easy vigor of a line,/ Where Denham's
strength, and Waller's sweetness join" *(Essay on Criticism,* ll.
360–61).

With the decline of Waller's reputation in the Romantic era
and afterwards, critics grew less enthusiastic about the worth of
such a quality in such a poet. Charles C. Clarke (in 1869)
describes one of Waller's poems as "a tissue of smooth and
musical mediocrity."[15] Edmund Gosse preferred to think of him
as "smooth" and "serried."[16] The maverick Ezra Pound in our
own century has fallen in with the trend visible in Clarke and
Gosse: "Waller . . . was a tiresome fellow. . . . His natural

talent is fathoms below My Lord Rochester's. BUT when he writes for music he is 'lifted'; but he was very possibly HOISTED either by the composer or by the general musical perceptivity of the time."[17]

B. Waller's Role in the Reform of English Verse—The Augustan View

It is, however, the corollary claim by Waller's contemporaries and by major figures in Augustan literature that has proved to be the major problem in literary criticism and literary history. What is his role in the two neoclassical programs of refining the language and developing the music of the couplet? A major intellectual experience of the seventeenth century, increasingly so after mid-century, was the sense of release from erroneous views ("false sentiments") in science and elsewhere, from outmoded methods of argument and obscure language, from clumsy, "low," and indelicate diction. This experience is prominent in the works of the major British philosophers— Bacon, Hobbes, Locke—and in the major poet of the Restoration, Dryden—and in the values, proceedings, and history of the Royal Society. Restoration literary awareness vibrates with self-gratulation on being more melodious, more correct, more refined than the Elizabethan and Jacobean past. And it became an "official" part of this awareness that Waller was instrumental in the progress made. Both great Dryden himself and the author (perhaps Francis Atterbury) of the Preface to *The Second Part of Mr. Waller's Poems* (1690) made unequivocal cases for Waller's significance. As noted earlier, Dryden constantly paid tribute to "Mr. Waller." In the "Epistle Dedicatory" of *The Rival Ladies* (1664), Dryden wrote, "The excellence and dignity of it [rhyme] were never fully known 'till Mr. Waller taught it; he first made writing easily an art; first showed us to conclude the sense most commonly in distichs, which, in the verse of those before him, runs on for so many lines together, that the reader is out of breath to overtake it."[18] Twenty-seven years later, after Waller's death, Dryden's praise was heightened ("Preface" to Walsh's *A Dialogue Concerning Women*): Referring to "Mr. Waller" as "the father of our English numbers," he added, "I hope the reader need not be told that Mr. Waller is only mentioned for honour's sake; that I am desirous of laying hold of his memory on all occasions, and thereby acknowledging to the world, that unless he had written, none of us could write."[19]

The author of the 1690 Preface mainly echoes Dryden's assertions:

The Tongue came into his [Waller's] hands, like a rough Diamond; he polish'd it first, and to that degree that all Artists since him have admired the Workmanship, without pretending to mend it. . . . He undoubtedly stands first in the List of Refiners, and for ought I know, last too. . . . [English poetry before Waller] was made up almost entirely of monosyllables. . . . Besides, their Verses ran all into one another, and hung together, throughout a whole Copy, like the *hook'd Attoms*, that compose a Body in *Des Cartes*. . . . Mr. *Waller* remov'd all these faults, brought in more Polysyllables, and smoother measures. . . . where-ever the natural stops of that [the verse] were, he contriv'd the little breakings of his sense so as to fall in with 'em. . . . Among other improvements we may reckon that of his Rhymes. . . . He had a fine Ear, and knew how quickly the Sense was cloy'd by the same round of chiming Words still returning upon it.[20]

Short comments by John Wilmot, Earl of Rochester and Samuel Butler (who were also Waller's contemporaries), some lengthier comments made over a period of years by John Dennis, and Pope's parody of Waller present the sharpest understanding of the nature of Waller's verse and of his "contribution." Rochester's appraisal is in "An Allusion to Horace," probably written in the mid-1670s and published in 1680.

> Waller, by nature for the bays designed,
> With force and fire and fancy unconfined,
> In panegyrics does excel mankind.
> He best can turn, enforce, and soften things
> To praise great conqu'rors, or to flatter Kings.[21]

An ironic, balanced judgment lies behind the surface praise. The effect is still one of praise, but judicious, perceptive praise, except for the overstated second line; it is precisely force and fire and fancy that post-Romantic readers think that Waller lacks. The term *by nature* in the first line suggests that it is not *by study* or effort that Waller wrote—certainly an effect that he intended to give. The question is not whether in fact Waller wrote easily or struggled through many revisions. It will perhaps remain always a question whether *unstudied ease* is achieved by

study or grace. Any one trying to write a poem in imitation of
Waller or Sedley quickly discovers the labors in some form of
easiness. Rochester means to note the naturalness and ease of the
product; or, to be precise, to note that the product suggests a
natural and easy talent. Also, he is sensitive to what was more
apparent to contemporaries than to the modern reader, the
happiness of Waller's "parts," his ease and felicity of courtesy
and language.

The series in line five describes Waller's poetic doings: *turn,
enforce, soften.* That line is perhaps the best critical sentence on
Waller. The three verbs with some accuracy describe his poetic
practice and excellence. *Turn* refers to the playing with
repeated ideas, words, images, and is but one of the whole
battery of rhetorical weapons Waller deployed. *Enforce*
describes the heightening of powers which he was ever seeking
(through applications, outdoing compliments, hyperboles, discoveries of honorific hieroglyphs) in the great, the beautiful, the
talented. And *soften* suggests the Lydian mode of his poems to
ladies and the concessions he made to feminine perspective as
well as his skill in minimizing the faults of the subjects of his
panegyrics. The last line grants Waller his excellence in
panegyric, but in the third the pun on *excel* implies that he
presents more fiction than truth. Also, the antithesis in the last
line, a favorite device of Waller himself, reminds the reader that
Waller's praise was fickle.

Although he began to publish his criticism when Waller's
reputation was near its height, John Dennis judged his poetry
with considerable detachment. Consider the following remarks
from *The Impartial Critick* (1693): "There is no Man who has a
greater Veneration from Mr. Waller than I have: . . . A man may
in many places of Mr. *Waller's* Works, see not only Wit, Spirit,
good Sence, but a happy and delicate turn of Thought, with
clearness, boldness, justness, sublimeness, and gallantry. For the
last of these Qualities, I know not whether he has been surpass'd
by any Writer in any Language." Dennis contrasts the "gallantry" of Voiture with Waller's, which "is more sprightly, more
shining, more bold, and more admirable. The *French*-man's, by
the Character of his Country, more supple, more soft, more
insinuating, and more bewitching."[22]   The word "gallant"
suggests at once epic or romantic forces (dashing, spirited, bold),
ornateness, delicacy of manner, and amatory strategies; it

synthesizes the qualities of the corpus of Waller's poems.

Dennis shared the common opinion that Waller "was the first who us'd our Ears to the Musick of a just Cadence." But Dennis also noted on several occasions that there is much "Prose in his [Waller's] Verse" as well as improprieties of diction, language, and image. Also, Dennis's gloss on Pope's tribute to Denham and Waller in the *Essay on Criticism* embodies a longer range or better view of classicism than Pope's: "Now he who is familiar with Homer, and intimate with *Virgil*, will not be extremely affected either with the Sweetness of *Waller*, or the Force of *Denham.* . . . I will not deny but that *Waller* has Sweetness, and *Denham* Force; but their good and their shining Qualities are so sophisticated and debauch'd with these modern Vices of Conceit and Point, and Turn, and Epigram, that 'tis impossible they can affect in an extraordinary manner those who have been long acquainted with the Ancients."[23] Pope's translation of the *Iliad* brought, curiously, these "modern Vices" into that poem, where the interest of the translator's art was at once to maximize rhetorical complexity and to sharpen moral point.

Dennis, however, can be called as witness, perhaps a reluctant witness, to prove that Waller succeeds in what was to Waller the highest goal of art. A friend had apparently asked Dennis whether the poem "To Amoret" *moved* him: "the Verses to *Amoret* move even the vulgar Passions in me, as they ought to do: It being impossible to take a Survey in them of Mr. *Waller's* Good-nature, and his Gratitude, without pitying and loving him."[24] One imagines Waller being pleased with that response.

Of Pope's several imitations of Waller, one stands out as an excellent bit of literary criticism: "Of A Lady Singing to Her Lute" was first published in 1717, but said to have been written when Pope was thirteen:

> Fair charmer cease, nor make your voice's prize
> A heart resign'd the conquest of your eyes:
> Well might, alas! that threaten'd vessel fail,
> Which winds and lightning both at once assail.
> We were too blest with these inchanting lays,
> Which must be heav'nly when an angel plays;
> But killing charms your lover's death contrive,
> Lest heav'nly musick should be heard alive.
> *Orpheus* could charm the trees, but thus a tree
> Taught by your hand, can charm no less than he;

> A poet made the silent wood pursue;
> This vocal wood had drawn the poet too.

In this revised form of the first couplet, Pope achieves the more Wallerian effects of smoother sense (more consonant ideas) and of turn accented by rhyme. The original read: "Fair charmer cease, nor add your tuneful breath/ T' o'ercome the slave your eyes have doom'd to Death."[25] The joint effect of sound and sight is not smoothly established, nor is there adequate yoking of their agency. But the revision is a perfect parody. The lines are made to carry the maximal amount of turn or balance consonant with the maximal smoothness. Thus: *prize* and *conquest; cease* and *resign'd; voice* and *eyes.* Or diagrammatically, *charmer, voice, eyes* versus *prize, heart, conquest* form not just a simple chiasmus, but a cross in this form (a = the lady and her powers, b = the lover defeated):

$$a\text{------}a\text{------}b$$
$$b\text{------}b\text{------}a$$

(In Puttenham's term, this is a complex *antimetabole.*) Pope plays at the same replication, balance, and ease in the last four lines. The Orpheus-poet appears in each line; *charmed trees* become *tree charming,* in perfect crisscross; and in the last couplet *poet moving wood* crosses into *wood moving the poet,* accompanied by a brightening effect of antithesis between Orpheus' *silent* wood and the *vocal* wood of the lady's lute.

The melodic strategies in Pope's parody are somewhat more difficult to isolate. The open vowels abound and constitute every rhyme. The rhymes are figured importantly into the pattern of turn and antithesis, just as the caesuras emphasize oppositions and replications. Alliteration and assonance are part of the sought-for melodiousness, but both function in a strategy of emphasis on echoes of sense: the sound echoes are echoes of ideas, almost literally *musical turns.* Consider the couplet where the *l* sounds keep ideas of *kill* and *lover* in the ear: "But killing charms your lover's death contrive,/ Lest heav'nly musick should be heard alive." Contrary to the absurd claim of the 1711 *Life* that Waller had first "introduced" the use of alliteration, Pope understood that Waller had explored a number of artistically challenging possibilities in the use of sound aligned with rhetoric and sense. Pope became the master of these possibilities.

Good reasons exist for considering Samuel Butler's criticism after Rochester's, Dennis's, and Pope's. For one, the criticism (although written before Butler's death in 1680, perhaps during the period 1667–69) was not published until 1759. For another, Pope's parody enables one to comprehend the full force of Butler's mainly hostile view of Waller (which bears some resemblance to Dennis's):

> There are two ways of Quibling, the one with words, and the other with Sense; Like the Figurae Dictionis, and Figurae Sententiae, in Rhetorique. The first is don by shewing Tricks with words of the Same Sounds, but Different Senses: And the other by expressing of Sense by Contradiction, and Riddle. Of this Mr. Waller, was the first most copious Author, and has so infected our modern writers of Heroiques with it, that they can hardly write any other way.

> [Of the two ways of quibbling] The first is already cried down, and the other as yet prevails; and is the only Elegance of our modern Poets, which easy Judges call *Easiness;* but having nothing in it but *Easiness,* and being never used by any lasting Wit, will in wiser Times fall to nothing of itself.[26]

By *quibbling with sense* Butler means using the favorite rhetorical devices of neoclassicism: antithesis, zeugma, turn— which have been illustrated often in the analyses of Chapters 2 and 3. Butler himself parodies the Wallerian turn, in the last passage quoted, by means of the repetition of *easiness.* But the value of his comment is in the connection of rhetorical play (quibbling with sense) with easiness. One of the innate qualities of those devices is a kind of smoothness or flow, especially in turn, zeugma, and antithesis, which is absent in some forms of pun and paradox. Puns often are forced; or they slow down or puzzle the reader or hearer. Thus, nearly all of Waller's puns are rendered unobtrusive, never causing the "sense" to stumble and disrupt the melody. Butler's insight into the ease realized in rhetoric of this kind reinforces the truth illustrated in Pope's parody that the intention of the Wallerian line is to maintain maximal rhetorical play *consonant with maximal smoothness.*[27] Waller may have succeeded too well in the easiness, as the common reader sees only the gleam of surface polish and little of the rhetoric and sense, and is only too eager to accept the

justness of Addison's parody. In *Tatler* 163, Ned Softly consults
Mr. Bickerstaff on alternate phrasings in his poem "To Mira."

> I fancy, when your song you sing,
> (Your song you sing with so much Art.)

or,

> I fancy, when your song you sing,
> You sing your song with so much Art.

Bickerstaff's reply is "Truly . . . the Turn is so natural either
way, that you have made me almost giddy with it." It is to be
noted (1) that Bickerstaff's reply is in the form of a graceful pun
on the word *turn*, and (2) that Addison's prose style (in elegance,
ease, melodiousness, and rhetorical devices) parallels Waller's in
verse.

C.   A Survey of Modern Opinion

The two late Victorians who concerned themselves in detail
with Waller are G. Thorn-Drury and Edmund Gosse. As Thorn-
Drury had almost no interest in the poetry, he devoted only the
last four and a half pages of the introduction to his edition to a
critical commentary on the poems. And Gosse was one of those,
so aptly described by James Sutherland, who saw the neoclassical
age "as a rather dull plain lying between two ranges of
Delectable Mountains."[28] Gosse would perhaps prefer his own
words: Waller led a revolt against Elizabethan poetry which
"shut it [poetry] in a cage for a hundred and fifty years." Or, in a
more elegant image, Gosse declared, "English poetry was a
widow who married Shakespeare for love, and now consented to
marry Waller for position." On the question of Waller's role in
developing the "classical couplet," Gosse made some sensible
points: "It is, of course, obvious that Waller could not 'introduce'
what had been invented, and admirably exemplified, by
Chaucer. But those who have pointed to smooth distichs
employed by poets earlier than Waller have not given sufficient
attention to the fact (exaggerated, doubtless, by critics arguing in
the opposite camp) that it was he who earliest made writing in
the serried couplet the habit and fashion."[29]

Gosse's statements find parallels in the judicious *A History of*

English Prosody by George Saintsbury: "let nobody interject any doubt about Waller's actual part in a certain rather questionable 'reform of our numbers.' The people who followed that reform believed in his part in it for a century and a half, and that is the point of importance. . . . More than half the modern readers who are indignant with 'Waller was smooth' are so because their ideal of smoothness and Pope's or Johnson's are two quite different things." Somewhat derivative of the 1690 Preface, Saintsbury's examination of the technique of the Wallerian couplet also deserves quotation: "Keeping the pause as close to the middle as possible naturally causes a slight opposition, or antithesis, of motion in the two halves, and this as naturally invites a slight antithesis of sense." But the verse is insipid, according to Saintsbury; "both measure and diction are flaccid; there is no throb, no quiver, no explosive and jaculative quality about them." And he furnished his own metaphor to place Waller in English poetry: "his genius prompted him continually in the direction of the smooth, stopped, antithetic couplet. He was, of course, not its Columbus; nobody was. It was only an island lying off the inhabited continent, which had been visited now and then, but never regularly colonized till, about his time, the chief seat of prosodic civilisation and government was transferred to it."[30]

In the 1930s there were three significant studies of Waller's place in the prosodic movement of the seventeenth century. Those by George Williamson and Ruth Wallerstein begin from different premises but make similar discoveries about the nature of "couplet rhetoric"; in the words of W. K. Wimsatt, the two discerned the following characteristics: "the sententious closure, the balanced lines and half-lines, the antithesis and inversion, the strict metric and accordingly slight but telling variations, the constantly close and tensile union of what are called musical with logical and rhetorical effects."[31] The same could be said of an earlier study, a Cambridge dissertation (1931) by Margaret Deas Cohen, a part of which is devoted to an analysis of Waller's style and the influences on it. From Fairfax's translation of Tasso Waller learned much: "all the mannerisms which give the air of modernity: — the regular couplet swing, the balancing of phrase with phrase, and word with word, the antithesis of line with line, and half line with half line, the contrasted simile, the frequent and colourless personification, all these are common to Fairfax

and Waller." Related refinements derive from the Latin elegiac
distich: "All that Ovid may have taught Waller is that in a closed
couplet points may be effectively and concisely made by the
balancing of half line with half line, either reinforcing each
other, or by contrast indicating the container of both: that
adjectives and nouns may be used in the same way: and that
zeugma is a useful construction when the sentence can have no
larger abiding place than one line. But in the contrast of half lines
Ovid is more often indicating the anomaly of the contrast in the
person or thing, Waller more often the reconciliation of the
contrast in them. He may also have strengthened Waller's native
habit of compliment."[32]

Ruth C. Wallerstein's "The Development of Rhetoric and
Metre of the Heroic Couplet, especially in 1625-1645" is a
detailed analysis of specific qualities of poets who wrote in or
influenced the development of the closed couplet. Stipulating
that the couplet "originated as a naturalization of the Latin
elegiac distich," she begins with the development before and at
the turn of the seventeenth century, in (1) Drayton's imitation of
Ovid, *England's Heroicall Epistles* (which had its English pred-
ecessors in translating or imitating Ovid), published in 1597, and
in (2) Fairfax's translation of Tasso, published in 1600. Both of
these, Wallerstein argues, demonstrate a definite if various
strategy of combined rhetorical and metrical balance. It is
difficult to do justice to her study in a brief summary. The
perceptions in it, supported by a complex of particularities, may
be generalized as follows: (a) the characteristics of the closed
couplet are observable in a number of writers from 1597 to 1646;
(b) attributing the achievement of the consummate closing of it
to any one writer is problematic or erroneous, as those writing in
the form (the little-known as well as the widely touted) share in
varying degrees a number of practices—as shown in statistics
concerning the placement of caesuras, the balance of half lines,
the number of monosyllables and polysyllables; (c) Michael
Drayton, Edward Fairfax, Ben Jonson, George Sandys, Viscount
Falkland, Waller, John Denham, Martin Lluelyn and others are to
be observed in the development. Jonson is seen as employing
most of the devices of the perfect closed couplet without having
the rigidity of that form as practiced afterwards. A peculiarity of
Wallerstein's study is a high claim for Falkland's verse, as
showing "a full and unflagging hold of the closed couplet design

and of the integration of its rhetoric and music and rapid energy and freedom." The two qualities assigned to Falkland—"rapid energy and freedom"—distinguish him from Waller, whose "'smoothness' is on the whole an evenness of tension beyond what we have seen in anyone else." Wallerstein uses extraordinarily sharp terms to delineate Waller's peculiarities, in a description of three of his poems: "Their oft-noted smoothness is dependent first upon the almost constant repetition of the twenty-syllable unit in the closed couplet, and upon the prevalent repetition of the half-line pattern with medial caesura (an element present also in Drayton and Sandys, and typical of Jonson and Falkland) and upon the flexible syllabication and the little variation in stress. All this is sustained in a way not quite found in any previous case we have been considering, by the unemphatic, direct, smooth-flowing, conversational ease of expression, deliberate and perfectly neatly defined, which makes every word duly weighty, though it prevents any word from attaining a thrilling emphasis."[33]

George Williamson's essay "The Rhetorical Pattern of Neoclassical Wit" begins with the admission, as in Gosse, Saintsbury, and others, that it is difficult to determine who the sole inventor of the neoclassical couplet was: The "urges" of it "were in the air, and manifested themselves occasionally in various poets, being most persistent in Waller. . . . the connecting link was less the couplet itself than the informing force of the couplet, which was a manner of saying things ultimately derived from Latin rhetoric." After illustrating the connection with Latin rhetoric, mainly by means of George Puttenham's *The Arte of English Poesie* (1589), Williamson concludes that Waller was "a consolidator of a poetic development and . . . the acknowledged leader of a restrictive movement. . . . Waller turned the balance from paradox to antithesis in the poetic wit which centered in contradiction." In contrast to the metaphysical poets, the wit depends "less upon startling reconciliations and more upon surprising oppositions. From the surprising opposition of ideas wit passed into verse as opposition of structure."[34]

These useful and objective analyses were followed by attacks from two prominent scholars. In *English Literature in the Earlier Seventeenth Century 1600–1660* (1945), Douglas Bush dispensed in few words with Waller, whose reputation has been "completely and irreparably eclipsed"—"the classicism of Waller and

Denham was only the ghost of Jonson's. . . . they were but superficial signs of a larger movement" of neoclassicism. The decline in verse was, according to Bush, paralleled in an attenuation of music: "There was in general a movement away from bold imaginative freedom towards regularity which was roughly parallel to the movement in verse associated with Waller and Denham; one representative of the new tendencies was Henry Lawes."[35]

F. R. Leavis, sensitive alike to the loss of "vitality" and an unfortunate shift in musical appeal from what he calls the "inner" to the "outer ear," had in an earlier study (1936) left Waller totally out of the line of wit (which, according to him, runs from Carew to Pope) and objected to Waller's bringing upper-crust social modes into art. Conceding that Waller was influential, he found the influence baleful: Waller's reform is "inseparable from a concept of 'Good Form,' . . . the ease, elegance and regularity favoured belong, we feel, to the realm of manners; the diction, gesture and deportment of the verse observe a polite social code; and the address is, as has been said already, to the 'outer ear'—to an attention that expects to dwell upon the social surface."[36]

Thus, shortly before mid-century, Waller's declined reputation fell further; or, if it had pulled up from a Victorian nadir, it fell again—to judge by the pronouncement of these two academic authorities on both sides of the Atlantic—and to judge also by Ezra Pound, a nonacademic transatlantic critic, whose views were mentioned earlier. According to these three, Waller was insignificant, superficially polite, and dull. It was time, to say the least, for "A Word for Waller" by F. W. Bateson in 1950,[37] for H. M. Richmond's perceptions of Waller's impressive relationships to European poetic tradition (considered in Chapter 2), and for two balanced book-length studies of Waller in the 1960s: Alexander Ward Allison's *Toward an Augustan Poetic: Edmund Waller's Reform of English Poetry* (1962) and Warren L. Chernaik's *The Poetry of Limitation: A Study of Edmund Waller* (1968).[38]

Allison presents four major propositions: (1) Waller "reveals . . . the deliquescence of the early seventeenth-century sensibility . . . anticipating the tone-quality of compliment in an age of 'taste.' " (2) Waller's "refinement" of the language consisted of elegance and preciousness of diction, periphrasis, the use of

Latinate words with etymological overtones, the preference for generalized epithets which nonetheless are selected to enhance pathos or sympathy, the use of a number of rhetorical devices (zeugma, turn, and the like) common to Ovid and Spenser, and the establishing of polite discourse as the model for the language of poetry. In several of these, Allison argues, the influence is Edmund Spenser, via Fairfax: Waller sought to "recreate Spenser's achievement without incurring Spenser's faults." (3) Waller's work illustrates the "metamorphosis of the Jacobean wit into the neoclassical. . . . The neoclassical wit is like the Jacobean in that it continues to perceive arresting relationships between things apparently unlike, distinguished from it in that it is as sensitive to differences as to similarities." (4) Allison's most original argument, indebted to modern linguistics, is that Waller's achievement was an "accommodation" of essentially foreign metrical patterns to the genius of the English language: "one means of domesticating the decasyllabic line in particular was to marry an iambic meter to the accentual and phrasal balance which had characterized a purely native poetry."[39]

Chernaik devotes his last chapter to the Augustan view of Waller as "Parent of English Verse." In Waller's verse Chernaik finds a strategy of the "well-plac'd word," a Latinate diction and syntax, Vergilian epithets and heightening of effects, a "concentration on technique as an end in itself," "elaborate patterns of parallel and contrasting elements," including, of course, the turn. "Waller's 'smoothness' is partly an evenness of tone: his effects are all muted, small-scale. Metrically his verse is regular and harmonious." (The reader must of course refer to that chapter for the wealth of supporting evidence and valuable bibliographic reference.)[40]

Both Allison and Chernaik end their studies with praise of Waller for developing potentialities in poetry which Dryden and Pope were to realize. And they do not find the development itself lacking in poetic interest.

III   *Waller's Art in Practice and Theory and His Place in Literary History*

At a social level, Waller's verse is tuned to normative values as well as to melody. He adapts a primitive understanding of poetry—as powerful sound—to an idealism he inherited from some Renaissance poets. A program of mythic bardic potency and an idealizing purpose suffer a diminution or dislocation when focussed on actual and immediate events within a small and well-informed society.

To put the matter another way, the balance which Waller praises Jonson for maintaining, the balance between art as imitative of the deformed actual world and as yet imitative of ideal principles, this Waller himself sacrifices in panegyric verse which attempts to use orphic powers to elevate the actual into the ideal. A question of sincerity arises; the resources of the myth become subject to "skeptical doubts." This problem, discussed in Chapter 3, parallels a spirit (or, more precisely, an anti-spirit) of demythologization which is the essence of the Enlightenment. The tone of such an art becomes that of the sophisticate—urbane, "rational," skeptical. Waller's infusing historical trivialities with orphic hieroglyphs nonetheless induced, consciously or unconsciously, precisely this tone, a detachment for which the Augustans had, to say the least, a relish.[41]

By Dryden's day, Waller's manner was a model of poetic self-understanding. The earlier part of this chapter presents the aesthetic principles implied or stated in his works, which principles are obviously the pattern of a fairly large part of English Augustan poetry. It is Waller's felicitous combination of these principles, as well as his artistry in the use of the couplet, that provides the elucidating context for Dryden's assertion, "unless he had written, none of us could write." One may summarize these principles in a few sentences: In poetry as in rhetoric, the concern is *moving* the auditors and coloring the subject (or that it is the poet's task to effect the acceptance of fictions); aggrandizing, idealizing, goldenizing are presumed to be proper goals. Except in amatory verse, and sometimes there, the "official" duty of the poet is an overstated didacticism; the poet is the guardian of public morals and, in his public personage, the model of propriety not only in private and political duties but also in piety. The social role implies a social manner, influenced by the French, of ease, elegance, and unstudied gracefulness. Ideas and expression are limited to modes of clarity, intelligibility, immediacy of cognition. All of these, which are nearly always present and often obtrusive in Waller, explain in part the high reputation he enjoyed for almost a century and a half.

The point to insist on is that Dryden and Pope (and many others in the seventeenth and eighteenth centuries) praised Waller because he did a number of things well. He wrote with a grace that disguised the art. The texture of his verse, when perfect, balances maximal smoothness with maximal rhetorical play. He was sly and civilized at once. He applied a musical instinct and a poetic cunning to a number of technical problems of his craft (diction, "numbers") and to his favorite intentions in art (to seduce, to magnify, to gild, to enhance, to discover powers).

He ought to stand in merit as a rare minor poet,[42] near to Herrick. But he does not, mainly because of a number of unfortunate, and in some cases, nonpoetic circumstances: his wealth, his compromising at certain times in politics, his plot and his shameless zeal to escape, the subjects he chose for some of his panegyrics (the Stuart kings), his becoming the official harbinger of an "age of prose." But most important for the modern reader, unaware of any of these circumstances, who picks up one of the score or so of great lyrics, is the easy simplicity of what appears to be idle song—or, in Chernaik's phrase, "mindless song." There is, instead of the immediately perceivable charm of Herrick, a surface of bland urbanity. The maximized smoothness, like a highly polished surface, succeeds too well and diverts one from the sense below. But, as represented in Chapters 2 and 3, ironic play and complexity of wit *do* work and charm, in many poems. As a craftsman in irony and nuance, as the crafty discoverer of truth-through-rhetoric, as a devotee of grace and ease who determined to make his verse harmonious and civilized—Waller deserved to be respected by Dryden and Pope and deserves to be read today.

Waller's contribution to the couplet was not in smoothing it, or closing it, or balancing it, or in developing in it strategies for rhyme, for alliteration, or for variation in poly- and monosyllables. Rather, it was in bringing the values mentioned in the last paragraph, along with a general concentration on refining rhetorical and musical possibilities, into couplet art. Dryden, Pope, Johnson, Goldsmith excel him, not simply because they continued a poetic tradition which he started, but because they bring energy and more powerful minds into the same craft. We must note the felicity, and the absence of greatness, of his achievement.

But ease in writing flows from art, not chance;
As those move easiest who have learned to dance.[43]

Notes and References

Chapter One

1. Quoted by John Aubrey, *Aubrey's Brief Lives*, ed. by Oliver L. Dick (London: Secker and Warburg, 1958), p. 310. Cited hereafter as *Brief Lives*.

2. *Poems, Etc. . . . The Eighth Edition . . . To Which Is Prefix'd The Author's Life* (London: Tonson, 1711), pp. iv–v. Cited hereafter as 1711 *Life*.

3. See the anecdotes about her in *The Poems of Edmund Waller*, ed. by G. Thorn-Drury (London: Routledge; New York: Dutton, n.d. [1905], I, lix, lx), cited hereafter as Thorn-Drury, and in the 1711 *Life*, vi.

4. One Edmund Waller assigned quarters in Lincoln's Inn was not the poet. See *Admissions from 1420 to 1799* in *The Records of the Honourable Society of Lincoln's Inn* (London, 1896), I. fol. 67b. In *The Black Books* (London, 1898), II, 277, there is a notice of admission on July 2, 1628, of Mr. John Bourcher "into the part of Mr. Edmond Waller's chamber." Waller's many recorded comments in parliamentary debate bespeak a knowledge of the law, as does his being chosen to deliver the case against Judge Crawley in the Long Parliament; but he himself said in the speech attacking Crawley that "it has not beene my happinesse to have the Law a part of my breeding"—*Mr. Waller's Speech in Parliament, At a conference of both Houses in the painted chamber. 6 Iuly 1641.* (London, 1641), p. 2. See Margaret Deas Cohen, "A Study of the Life and Poetry of Edmund Waller," Diss. Cambridge University 1931, p. 6., cited hereafter as Cohen.

5. *Debates of the House of Commons, 1667–1694, Collected by Anchitell Grey* (London: Henry and Cave, 1763), I,354–55, cited hereafter as Grey's Debates.

6. *Members of Parliament: Part I. Parliaments of England, 1213–1702* (London, 1878), pp. 450–552. There is some uncertainty whether Waller sat in the parliament of James II. The returns just cited show an Edmund Waller elected to the House; and Grey's Debates (VII, 357, 364–65) record brief speeches by "Mr. Waller." But according to Margaret Deas Cohen, "the two sessions of 1678 were [the poet's] last in Parliament," p. 110. The Waller of the returns and the Debates could be the poet's son Edmund. Among the family papers (which Major W. R. Waller kindly allowed me to read) there is a letter

dated April 6, 1685, from the Earl of Sunderland to the poet; the Earl takes note of Waller's son's standing *for Buckinghamshire* in the election to the House. He may have failed, and either he or his father may have been named to represent Saltash, Cornwall. The evidence for assuming the poet to be the M.P. is that the brief comments recorded by Grey sound like Waller's in the parliament of 1661–79 and that early biographical records and several poems suggest a friendly relationship and routine communication with James II when he was king. Dr. John Campbell, who looked into the records with some care, says in *Biographia Britannica* (London, 1766), VI, Pt. 2, 4111–12n., that Waller was also returned in the third parliament of Charles II (1679–80).

7. See, e.g.: the Preface to *The Second Part of Mr. Waller's Poems* (London, 1690), sig. A5[r]; 1711 *Life*, x; and Elijah Fenton, "Observations on some of Mr. Waller's Poems," *The Works of Edmund Waller, Esq.r, in Verse & Prose* (London, 1729), pp. iv, viii.

8. *The Life of Edward Earl of Clarendon . . . Written by Himself* (Oxford: Clarendon Press, 1759), p. 25, cited hereafter as *Life of Clarendon*.

9. Cohen, p. 12, and *Cobbett's Parliamentary History of England* (London, 1807), II, 463, 467. See also James Arthur Steele, who doubts the Waller whose words are recorded is the poet: "A Biography of Edmund Waller," Diss. University of London 1965, pp. 61ff., cited hereafter as Steele.

10. *Analytical Index to the Series of Records Known as the Remembrancia Preserved Among the Archives of the City of London. A.D. 1579–1664* (London, 1878), pp. 319–20 and n. See also Steele, 65–80.

11. See Kurt Weber, *Lucius Cary: Second Viscount Falkland* (N.Y., 1940). and J.A.R. Marriott, *The Life and Times of Lucius Cary Viscount Falkland* (New York and London, 1907).

12. *Life of Clarendon*, 24–25; 1711 *Life*, xi, xii.

13. "Waller," *Lives of the English Poets*, ed. G. B. Hill (Oxford: Clarendon Press, 1905), I, 252, cited hereafter as Johnson's *Lives of the Poets*.

14. For information about his financial gains, see Cohen, p. 83; on his courting many ladies, see 1711 *Life*, xiv; the rather stuffy and proper Symonds D'Ewes recorded in his parliamentary diary a graphic account of Waller's alleged amours: "having been a widower many years, he was so extremely addicted and given to the use of strange women as it did for the most part alter his very countenance, and make him look as if his face had been parboiled, being naturally of a very pleasing and well-tempered complexion"—British Library, Harl. MS. 165. fol. 144.

15. *Essays and Verses About Books* (New York, 1926), pp. 47–57.

16. *The History of England* (London, 1762), V, 351.

17. Printed in *Memoirs, Illustrative of the Life and Writings of John Evelyn*, ed. by William Bray (London, 1818), II, 49.

18. *Note Book of Sir John Northcote*, ed. by A.H.A. Hamilton (London, 1877), pp. 85–86.

19. *The Journal of Sir Simonds D'Ewes. From the First Recess of the Long Parliament to the Withdrawal of King Charles from London*, ed. W. H. Coates (New Haven, 1942), pp. 94–95.

20. Sir Ralph Verney, *Notes on Proceedings in the Long Parliament, Temp. Charles I*, ed. John Bruce (London, 1845), p. 181.

21. Edward Hyde, First Earl of Clarendon, *The History of the Rebellion and Civil War: England* (Oxford: Clarendon Press, 1816), II, 316, cited hereafter as Clarendon's *History*.

22. See 1711 *Life*, xxiii–xxiv; and *Journals of the House of Commons*, II, 750a; see also Steele, 224–25.

23. Clarendon's *History*, II, 316.

24. Quoted by Thorn-Drury, I, xlv.

25. Clarendon's *History*, II, 325.

26. *Mr. Wallers Speech in the House of Commons, On Tuesday the fourth of July, 1643* (London, 1643).

27. *Biographia Britannica*, VI, Pt. 2, 4108.

28. See Clarendon's *History*, II, 322, 325; the 1711 *Life*, xxvii; and Bodley MS. 62, Part I, fol. 111–12, printed in J. S. Sanford, *Studies and Illustrations of the Great Rebellion* (London, 1858), pp. 563–64.

29. Clarendon's *History*, II, 330.

30. See *Journals of the House of Commons*, II, 166b, 169b, 172b, 173b, 230b, 240b, 281b, 283, 284b.

31. D'Ewes records in House debate of May 15, 1644, Sir William Waller's presentation of a request for exile for Edmund—British Library, Harl. MS. 166, fol. 61b.

32. *Life of Clarendon*, p. 25.

33. John Evelyn, *Memoirs*, I, 207–54. See also Ella T. Riske, "Waller in Exile," *Times Literary Supplement* (October 13, 1932), p. 734, and Cohen, 80–87.

34. 1711 *Life*, xl.

35. See Aubrey, *Brief Lives*, pp. 310, 309, 156. P. R. Wikelund, " 'Thus I passe my time in this place': An Unpublished Letter of Thomas Hobbes," *English Language Notes*, 6 (1969), 263–68. Paul H. Hardacre, "A Letter from Edmund Waller to Thomas Hobbes," *Huntington Library Quarterly*, 2 (1948), 431–33.

36. On the pardon see *Journals of the House of Commons*, VII, 44 (November 27, 1651). On the permit and protective order see *Public Record Office, Callendar of State Papers, Domestic Series, Warrants from the Council of State*, May 27, 1651, and March 6, 1656.

37. I can find no earlier report of the anecdote than Gilles Ménage, *Ménagiana ou Les Bons Mots* (Paris, 1715), II, 46–47.

38. *Life of Clarendon*, 25.

39. Grey's Debates, I, 2, 128, 140, 160, 220; II, 33; III, 178.

40. Grey's Debates, I, 128; III, 302; V, 136.

41. *History of My Own Time* (Dublin, 1724), I, 219.

42. *Works of Robert Boyle* (London, 1744), V, 556-57.

43. British Library, Egerton MS. 922, fol. 27.

44. For two stories regarding conversations with James II, see 1711 *Life*, lii.

45. *Reports of the Royal Commission on Historical Manuscripts*, VI, 367b.

46. *Lives of the Poets*, I, 272; see 1711 *Life*, xlvii.

47. See Thomas Birch, *History of the Royal Society* (1756-57; facsimile repr. London, 1968), I, 8, 12, 23, 241-43, 499-500; III, 191; IV, 129. And Ella T. Riske, "Dryden and Waller as Members of the Royal Society," *PMLA*, 46, (1931), 951-54.

48. *Reports of the Royal Commission on Historical Manuscripts*, VI, 365b.

49. "Preface to Walsh's *Dialogue Concerning Women,*" *The Works of John Dryden*, ed. Sir Walter Scott, 2nd ed. (Edinburgh, 1821), XVIII, 5.

50. Thorn-Drury, I, lxix; see Grey's Debates, V, 155.

Chapter Two

1. See Henry Lawes *et al.*, *Select Ayres and Dialogues* (London, 1659), pp. 17, 51. And "The Second Book" of the same (London, 1669), pp. 12, 14, 36, 43.

2. Warren Chernaik, *The Poetry of Limitation*, pp. 115ff. employs the term panegyric for the large number of Waller's poems of praise.

3. See Brendan O Herir's editing of Waller's poem on Paul's in Appendix B of *Expans'd Hieroglyphicks: A Critical Edition of Sir John Denham's Coopers Hill* (Berkeley and Los Angeles, 1969), also p. 14. See the same author's "The Early Acquaintance of Denham and Waller," *Notes and Queries*, 211 (1966), 19-23. For information concerning the genre of the painter poem, see Henry B. Wheatley's learned note in *The Diary of Samuel Pepys*, VI, 96n; and *Poems on Affairs of State*, ed. George deF. Lord (New Haven and London, 1963), I, 20-156.

4. Quoted by George Williamson, *The Proper Wit of Poetry* (London, 1951), pp. 55, 104.

5. *Minor Poets of the Seventeenth Century*, ed. by R. G. Howarth (1931; repr. London & New York, 1969), pp. 123-24.

6. The term "application" had a related designation in pulpit oratory of Waller's day, in the general sense of the relating of the scriptural to the contemporary, and in a specific sense "in reference to 'the redemption purchased by Christ,'" *OED*. See W. Fraser Mitchell, *English Pulpit Oratory from Andrewes to Tillotson: A Study of Its Literary Aspects* (London and New York, 1932), pp. 93ff., 369.

7. All quotations of Waller's poems are from G. Thorn-Drury's

edition (London and New York, [1905]). First published in 1893, this text of Waller's poems is faulty. Thorn-Drury states in his preface that he had "adopted, as far as practicable, the text of the edition of 1686, the last published during the poet's life." Yet he used a nineteenth-century edition as copy-text. Thorn-Drury's consultation of early printings seem to have been casual at best; he incorporated some variant readings and referred to some in notes. See the introductory paragraph of "Primary Sources" in the bibliography printed below.

8. Chernaik, *The Poetry of Limitation*, p. 86.

9. Thorn-Drury, I, xxviii.

10. Thorn-Drury, I, xxiv.

11. 1711 *Life*, xv–xvi.

12. H. M. Richmond, *The School of Love: The Evolution of the Stuart Love Lyric* (Princeton, 1964), p. 145; and Chernaik, *The Poetry of Limitation*, p. 81.

13. *The Arte of English Poesie*, ed. by Gladys D. Willcock and Alice Walker (Cambridge, 1936), pp. 203–04, 208. See also Chernaik, pp. 214–18.

14. *Characters and Passages from Note-Books*, ed. by A. R. Waller (Cambridge, 1908), 90, 414–15.

15. See, e.g., Chernaik, *The Poetry of Limitation*, pp. 110–13; Williamson, *The Proper Wit of Poetry*, p. 106; Allison, *Toward an Augustan Poetic*, pp. 54–55.

16. See "Introduction" to *Leviathan:* "when I shall have set down my own reading orderly, and perspicuously, the pains left another, will be only to consider, if he also find not the same in himself."

17. See Richmond's brilliant tracing of Waller's literary connections in *The School of Love*.

18. Chernaik, *The Poetry of Limitation*, p. 98.

19. See the excellent commentaries on this poem by Earl Miner, *The Cavalier Mode from Jonson to Cotton* (Princeton, 1971), pp. 39–41; Richmond, "The Fate of Edmund Waller," *South Atlantic Quarterly*, 60 (1961), 238; and Chernaik, *The Poetry of Limitation*, pp. 107–09.

20. *The School of Love*, pp. 59–64.

21. "The Fate of Edmund Waller," p. 236. See also his discussion of the poem in *The School of Love*, pp. 214–16.

22. James Boswell, *Life of Johnson*, ed. by R. W. Chapman (Oxford Standard Authors: London, 1953), p. 69.

23. Richmond, "The Fate of Edmund Waller," p. 234.

24. Ellipsis in the original. Richmond, *The School of Love*, pp. 196–97.

25. Aubrey, *Brief Lives*, pp. 309–10.

26. For a detailed study of this popular interest, see Maren-Sofie Røstvig, *The Happy Man: Studies in the Metamorphoses of a Classical Ideal 1600–1700* (Oslo, 1951).

27. See Miner's *The Cavalier Mode*, pp. 21–23.

Chapter Three

1. This poem was written after the birth of two or more of her children, four being born by 1640: see line 54, "For which so oft the fertile womb is vexed." This poem is remarkable for the image used to describe the effect of her station and character on would-be lovers: "She saves the lover, as we gangrenes stay,/ By cutting hope, like a lopped limb away."

2. This was written after the birth of her fourth child and after the Bishops' Wars had begun or when the civil war was threatening: "Fair Venus! in thy soft arms/ The God of Rage confine."

3. There is little evidence extant to suggest any prominence at court; see Cohen, 27.

4. *The Poetry of Limitation,* p. 136n.

5. "Observations," p. iii. See note 7, Chapter 1.

6. *Memoirs* (London, 1818), I, 234.

7. See "The Early Acquaintance of Denham and Waller," *Notes and Queries,* 211 (1966), 22; and *Expans'd Hieroglyphicks: A Critical Edition of Sir John Denham's Coopers Hill* (Berkeley and Los Angeles, 1969), Appendix B. Hereafter cited as *Expans'd Hieroglyphicks.*

8. That Waller was aware of the ambiguity is suggested by an account and interpretation of debate in Commons given by Christopher Hill in *The Century of Revolution 1603-1714* (Edinburgh, 1961), p. 66: "In 1641 Strafford was impeached, among other charges, for subverting the fundamental laws of the Kingdom. The Commons were just about to vote the charge when the witty and malicious Edmund Waller rose and, with seeming innocence, asked what the fundamental laws of the kingdom were. There was an uneasy silence. No one dared attempt a definition which would have divided the heterogeneous majority. . . . The situation was saved by a lawyer who leapt to his feet to say that if Mr. Waller did not know what the fundamental laws of the kingdom were, he had no business to be sitting in the house."

9. *Expans'd Hieroglyphicks,* p. 14. The information about texts is taken from pages 48, 91-162, 110n. The lines of the poem quoted are from pages 93-94. Appendix B, pages 276-83, includes an annotated reprinting of Waller's poem. See also the valuable comments on critical interpretation of seventeenth-century verse in the section "Nature's Emblems," pp. 16-24.

10. *The Poetry of Limitation,* pp. 172ff.

11. I am indebted to Chernaik's thorough study of this poem in *The Poetry of Limitation,* pp. 153ff.

12. See Chernaik's discussion of the term "protector" in *The Poetry of Limitation,* p. 161.

13. Chernaik denotes the technique *occupatio;* Pierre Legouis insists it is *praeterito,* review of Chernaik's *Poetry of Limitation, Études Anglaises,* XXII, 314-15.

14. Waller used the term, perhaps ironically, in defending his falling away from the religious mission of the zealots of the Long Parliament; see note 26, Chapter 1.

15. *The Poetry of Limitation*, p. 160.

16. Waller "frequently waited on the Usurper, and, as he often declar'd, observ'd him to be very well read in the *Greek* and *Roman* story"—1711 *Life*, p. xliii.

17. Cohen, p. 249.

18. *Leviathan*, ed. by Michael Oakeshott (Oxford, 1960), pp. 129-32. *Leviathan* was first published in 1651, four years before the "Panegyric."

19. Cf. Chernaik, *The Poetry of Limitation*, p. 161.

20. For further evidence beyond the salient points of the poem, see Grey's Debates, IV, 28.

21. See the valuable study by Joseph A. Mazzeo, "Cromwell as Davidic King," *Reason and the Imagination: Studies in the History of Ideas 1600-1800*, ed. by Mazzeo (London, 1962).

22. "Edmund Waller's Fitt of Versifying . . . ," *PQ*, 49 (1970), 91.

23. *The Cavalier Mode*, pp. 177-79.

24. *The Cavalier Mode*, p. 36.

25. On the puritan experience as gnostic, see Eric Voegelin, *The New Science of Politics* (Chicago, 1952). I am aware that there is a strong counterview to my response to Waller's complimentary symbolism. See, for examples, Gerard Reedy, "Mystical Politics: The Imagery of Charles II's Coronation" and Paul J. Korshin, "Figural Change and the Survival of Tradition in the Later Seventeenth Century," in *Studies in Change and Revolution: Aspects of Intellectual History 1640-1800*, ed. Paul J. Korshin (Menston, 1972), pp. 19-42, 99-128. Father Reedy finds comparisons of Charles to Christ as evidence of a reasserted but dying "noumenal sense." In the company of major Anglican and Catholic thinkers, however, Eric Voegelin takes note of distinct kinds of noumenal experience and symbolization, not all of which were considered intelligible or beneficial to human life. Consider how St. Irenaeus and Jonathan Swift distinguish their faith from gnostic madness.

26. *England in the Reign of Charles II*, 2nd edition (London, 1967), p. 453.

27. *Letters from Orinda* [Katharine Phillips] *to Poliarchus* (London, 1705), p. 206.

28. Paul H. Hardacre, "A Letter from Edmund Waller to Thomas Hobbes," *Huntington Library Quarterly*, 11 (1948), 431-33.

29. 1711 *Life*, viii-ix.

30. *The Cavalier Mode*, pp. 30-33.

31. Miner (*Cavalier Mode*, pp. 26-27n.) and Richmond *(The School of Love*, p. 64) comment on Marvell's echoing of Waller.

32. See George deF. Lord, *Poems on Affairs of State*, (New Haven,

1963) I, 20-21; Ephim G. Foegel, "Salmons in Both, or Some Caveats for Canonical Scholars," *Bulletin of the New York Public Library*, 63 (1959), 223-36; 292-308; and Chernaik, p. 192n.

33. *England in the Reign of Charles II*, 2nd. ed. (London, 1967), pp. 287-88.

34. "The Second Advice to a Painter" begins "Nay *Painter*, if thou dar'st designe that Fight/Which *Waller* only Courage had to write." See *Andrew Marvell: Complete Poetry*, ed. by George deF. Lord (New York, 1968), p. 117 and n.

35. *The Poetry of Limitation*, pp. 172-202.

36. *Toward an Augustan Poetic*, p. 13.

37. See two books which have been especially useful in this study: Ruth Nevo, *The Dial of Virtue: A Study of Poems on Affairs of State in the Seventeenth Century* (Princeton, 1963); and C. V. Wedgewood, *Poetry and Politics under the Stuarts* (Cambridge, 1960).

38. Thorn-Drury, II, 101, 111.

39. "The Evolution of Neoclassical Poetics: Cleveland, Denham, and Waller as Poetic Theorists," *Eighteenth-Century Studies*, 2 (1968), 135.

40. See J. A. Mazzeo, "Cromwell as Davidic King," pp. 29-32.

41. "To Sir William Davenant," *The Complete Works in Verse and Prose of Abraham Cowley*, ed. by A. B. Grosart (repr. New York, 1967), I, 144.

42. Commenting on this quality in Waller, Samuel Johnson quotes Roger Ascham on wits as *"open flatterers and privy mockers" (Lives*, I, 280).

43. *A Short View of Tragedy*, (London, 1693), p. 79.

44. Johnson's error is corrected by C. Lawrence Ford, "Waller," *Notes and Queries*, 9th Series, 4 (1899), 11.

45. *A Short View of Tragedy*, (London, 1693), p. 79.

46. See Allison's comments on the human interest given Waller's seascapes, *Toward an Augustan Poetic*, pp. 29-31.

47. See Waller's remarks in Commons: "In all my reading I could never find, but they that were superior at sea, make any conqueror weary of the War, in this part of the World. We were superior both to *Spain* and *France*, and made them weary of War with us," Grey's Debates, V, 90-91.

48. "Preface to the Fables," in *Essays of John Dryden*, ed. by W. P. Ker (New York, 1961), II, 247.

49. See Pope's *Essay on Man*, IV, 363-68:

> Self-love but serves the virtuous mind to wake,
> As the small pebble stirs the peaceful lake;
> The center moved, a circle straight succeeds,
> Another still, and still another spreads;
> Friend, parent, neighbor, first it will embrace;
> His country next; and next all human race.

Chapter Four

1. Thorn-Drury, I, lxxiii.

2. For a contemporary restatement of the traditional view of Orpheus, see John Oldham's "Horace's Art of Poetry, Imitated in English," *The Poems of John Oldham*, introd. by Bonamy Dobrée ([Carbondale], [1960]), p. 163. Fenton elaborates on the classical background of the myth, in Horace, Ovid, and Vergil—see "Observations," xxi-xxv. See also "Cities Their Lutes, and Subject Hearts Their Strings" in Ruth Nevo's *The Dial of Virtue*, pp. 20ff; and the survey of mimetic theories and pragmatic (or, in Waller's term, orphic) theories in M. H. Abrams, *The Mirror and the Lamp: Romantic Theory and Critical Tradition* (New York, 1953).

3. Milton's sonnet "Captain or Colonel, or Knight in Arms" borrows from the Cavalier arsenal arguments on the power of verse (his examples being a bit more recondite than theirs) and abandons for the moment the usual view of the poet as inspired communicator or as seer. The humor is that the goal in this case was to have a real "rhetorical" or "Orphic" influence in the real world, upon Cavaliers, who might be expected to be influenced when talked to in their own way.

4. "The Defence of Poesie," in *The Complete Works of Sir Philip Sidney*, ed. by Albert Feuillerat (Cambridge, England, 1923), III, 10.

5. Likening Jonson's love of his works to a fondness for one's offspring, Carew wrote, with bluntness: "Though one hand form them, and though one brain strike/ Souls into all, they are not alike." And he concludes, urging Jonson to stop his quarrel with the production of the play and see that he has failed: "the quarrel lies/ Within thine own verge: then let this suffice,/ The wiser world doth greater thee confess/ Than all men else, than thyself only less."

6. On the French influence, see J. W. H. Atkins, *English Literary Criticism: 17th and 18th Centuries* (Methuen: London, 1950), pp. 4-32, 45ff. The poet Thomas Gray thought of Waller and Pope as in a school of French verse; see René Wellek, *The Rise of English Literary History* (Chapel Hill, 1941), p. 165. On the problem in art created by the ideas of Ramus, see W. K. Wimsatt, Jr., and Cleanth Brooks, *Literary Criticism: A Short History* (New York, 1957), 223ff.

7. Thorn-Drury, II, 188.

8. See J. W. H. Atkins, *English Literary Criticism*, pp. 4-32.

9. *The Works of Virgil*, tr. by John Dryden (London, 1697), sig. °°4^r. See also Pope's quotation of this in Joseph Spence, *Observations, Anecdotes, and Characters of Books and Men*, ed. by James M. Osborne (Oxford, 1966), I, 196 and n.

10. Thorn-Drury, I, lxxiv.

11. *The Critical Works of John Dennis*, ed. by E. N. Hooker (Baltimore, 1939), I, 365.

12. *Brief Lives*, p. 308, emphasis added.

13. Wellek, *The Rise of English Literary History*, p. 35.

14. Quotations of Dryden's works are from W. P. Ker, *Essays of John Dryden*, (New York, 1961), I, 7, 35, 169; II, 28–29.

15. *The Poetic Works of Edmund Waller and Sir John Denham* (Edinburgh, 1869), p. vii.

16. "Edmund Waller," *Encylopedia Britannica*, 11th edition.

17. *ABC of Reading* (New Haven, 1934), pp. 142–43.

18. Ker, *Essays of John Dryden*, I, 7.

19. *The Works of Dryden*, 2nd ed., ed. by Sir Walter Scott (Edinburgh, 1821), XVIII, 5.

20. *The Second Part of Mr. Waller's Poems* (London, 1690), sig. A3^v-A4^r, A5^v-A6^r, A7^r.

21. *The Complete Poems of John Wilmot, Earl of Rochester*, ed. by David M. Vieth (New Haven and London, 1968), p. 123.

22. *The Critical Works of John Dennis*, I, 13–14.

23. Ibid., I, 14, 24–28; II, 384; I, 408.

24. Ibid., II, 401–02.

25. See Alexander Pope, *Minor Poems*, ed. by Norman Ault and John Butt (London and New Haven, repr. Norwich, 1964), p. 7 and n.

26. *Characters and Passages from Note-Books*, ed. by A. R. Waller (Cambridge, England, 1908), pp. 414–15, 90.

27. I do not intend to improve on, or reapply, Samuel Holt Monk's formula (nor Leibnitz's, which it may echo) that, "At its best, Jacobean poetry unites the maximum of complexity with the maximum of organization, so that no matter how subtle, penetrating, ambiguous, witty, passionate, and imaginative it may be, it is always and in all its parts functional, purposive, organic"—"From Jacobean to Augustan," *Southern Review*, 7 (1941–42), 366. Rather I am trying to define the essential quality of verse which, to Monk, in comparison to what one may call High Jacobean or High Donnean, seemed "flat and thin," p. 366. See Brendan O Herir's comments on the tendency to read seventeenth-century poets as disinherited sons of Donne in his review of Chernaik in *Modern Philology*, 68 (1970–71), 100–04.

28. James Sutherland, *A Preface to Eighteenth Century Poetry* (1948; repr. Oxford, 1958), p. 2.

29. *From Shakespeare to Pope*, 40, 101–02; "Edmund Waller," *Encyclopedia Britannica*, 11th Edition.

30. George Saintsbury, *A History of English Prosody* (London, 1908), II, 275, 280, 282–83, 286.

31. "Rhetoric and Poems," in *The Verbal Icon: Studies in the Meaning of Poetry* (University of Kentucky Press, 1954), p. 175.

32. Cohen, pp. 225–26, 232.

33. *Publications of the Modern Language Association*, 50 (1935), 166–209. William B. Piper, who has extended Wallerstein's analyses, considers Waller as playing a small but important role in the

development of the couplet: "We may say, indeed, that he achieved an excessive correctness of versification to express an excessive politeness of address" — *The Heroic Couplet* (Press of Case Western Reserve University, 1969), p. 90; see also pp. 83-89, 258-72.

34. *Modern Philology*, 33 (1935), 55-81.

35. (1945; repr. New York, 1952), pp. 166, 165, 169, 102. Ezra Pound presents an altogether different view of the state of music and its relationship to poetry; see note 17, above.

36. *Revaluation: Tradition and Development in English Poetry* (1936; repr. New York, 1947), p. 113; see also pp. 30, 33, 101, 112, 114.

37. In *English Poetry: A Critical Introduction* (London, 1950), 165-74.

38. These books and Earl Miner's *The Cavalier Mode* (1971) have enabled a sympathetic and informed reading of Waller.

39. Allison, pp. 4-23, 24-46, 59, 71.

40. *The Poetry of Limitation*, pp. 203-25.

41. See Chernaik for implications, noted in Chapter 3, between Waller's panegyrics and Augustan mock epic, *The Poetry of Limitation*, pp. 172-202.

42. See V. de Sola Pinto's review of Chernaik in *Notes and Queries*, 214 (1969), 391: "This useful study [by Chernaik] . . . completes the process by which he [Waller] is re-established as a minor poet of considerable merit and of very great historical interest."

43. Alexander Pope, *The Second Epistle of the Second Book of Horace*, ll. 178-79. See also his *Essay on Criticism*,. ll. 362-63.

Selected Bibliography

PRIMARY SOURCES

There has been no edition of Waller's poems since G. Thorn-Drury's (London: Lawrence & Bullen; New York: Charles Scribner's Sons, 1893), which has been reprinted in two volumes in the Muses' library. The citations in this study are to a 1905 reprint, cited below. It has been announced in several places for a number of years that Professor P. R. Wikelund is preparing an edition of Waller's poems. See Note 7, Chapter 2, above.

AUBREY, JOHN. *Aubrey's Brief Lives.* Ed. Oliver L. Dick. London: Secker and Warburg, 1958.

Cobbett's Parliamentary History of England, Vol. 2. London: Hansard, 1807.

Debates of the House of Commons, 1667-1694, Collected by Anchitell Grey. 10 vols. London: Henry and Cave, 1763.

HYDE, EDWARD (Earl of Clarendon). *The History of the Rebellion and Civil Wars in England.* 3 vols. Oxford: Clarendon Press, 1816.

———. *The Life of Edward Earl of Clarendon . . . Written by Himself.* Oxford: Clarendon Press, 1759.

Poems to the Memory of that Incomparable Poet Edmund Waller Esquire. By Several Hands. London: Knight and Saunders, 1688.

WALLER, EDMUND. *Mr. Wallers Speech in Parliament, at a Conference of Both Houses in the Painted Chamber. 6 Iuly 1641.* London: Abel Roper, 1641.

———. *Mr. Wallers Speech in the House of Commons, on Tuesday the Fourth of July, 1643.* London: G. Dexter, 1643.

———. "On the Marriage of Sir John Denham." *A Little Ark: Containing Sundry Pieces of Seventeenth-Century Verse.* Edited by G. Thorn-Drury. London: Dobell, 1921. P. 33.

———. *Poems, Etc. . . . The Eighth Edition . . . To Which Is Prefix'd The Author's Life.* London: Jacob Tonson, 1711.

———. *The Poems of Edmund Waller.* 2 vols. Edited by G. Thorn-Drury. London: Routledge; New York: Dutton, n.d. [1905]. (The Muse's Library).

———. *The Second Part of Mr. Waller's Poems. Containing His Alterations of the Maids Tragedy and Whatever of His Is Yet Unprinted.* London: Tho. Bennet, 1690.

——. *A Speech Made by Master Waller Esquire, in the Honorable House of Commons, Concerning Episcopacie, Whether It Should Be Committed or Rejected.* [London]: July 3, 1641.

——. *The Works of Edmund Waller Esqʳ. in Verse and Prose.* Edited by Elijah Fenton. London: J. Tonson, 1729.

——. *A Worthy Speech Made in the House of Commons This Present Parliament, 1641.* London: John Nicholson, 1641.

——. and others. *Pompey the Great. Translated out of French by Certain Persons of Honour.* London: H. Herringman, 1664. The first act is Waller's.

——. and Sidney Godolphin. *The Passion of Dido for Aeneas.* London: 1658.

SECONDARY SOURCES

ALLISON, ALEXANDER WARD. *Toward an Augustan Poetic: Edmund Waller's "Reform" of English Poetry.* [Lexington], University of Kentucky Press: 1962. An essay on Waller's role in the development of neoclassical verse.

The Ashley Library: A Catalogue of Printed Books, Manuscripts and Autograph Letters Collected by Thomas James Wise. London: Privately Printed, 1925, VII, 183–196. Notes on Waller's works and Walleriana; reproductions of title pages.

BATESON, F. W. "A Word for Waller." *English Poetry: A Critical Introduction.* London: Longmans, 1950. An intelligent and influential essay.

BUSH, DOUGLAS. *English Literature in the Earlier Seventeenth-Century 1600–1660.* 1945; repr. New York: Oxford University Press, 1952. There is a short bibliography of primary and secondary works, pp. 602–03.

[CAMPBELL, JOHN]. "Edmund Waller." *Biographia Britannica.* London: W. Innys, 1766. VI, Pt. 2, 4099–4115. An intelligent and fairly scrupulous biography.

"A Catalogue of a Collection of the Works of Edmund Waller." *The Oldenburgh House Bulletin,* No. 1. Tunbridge Wells: Courier, 1934. Contains a few bits of valuable information about editions and Walleriana.

CHERNAIK, WARREN L. *The Poetry of Limitation: A Study of Edmund Waller.* New Haven and London: Yale University Press, 1968. The fullest modern study.

CHEW, BEVERLY. "The First Edition of Waller's Poems." *The Bibliographer,* 1 (1902), 296–303. Reprinted in *Essays and Verses about Books.* New York, 1926. An analysis of four issues dated 1645.

COHEN, MARGARET DEAS. "A Study of the Life and Poetry of Edmund Waller." Unpublished diss. Cambridge University, 1931. A valuable study, especially of the life of Waller, with a large bibliography and appendices concerned with his letters, parliamentary activities, and speeches.

DICKINSON-BROWN, ROGER M. "The Art of Edmund Waller: A Technical and Prosodic Analysis." Unpublished diss. Syracuse University, 1976. An analysis of meter, alliteration, rhetorical figuration, and structure.

G[OSSE], E[DMUND]. "Edmund Waller." *Encylopedia Britannica*. 11th ed.

——. From Shakespeare to Pope. 1885; repr. New York: Franklin, 1968. A representative Victorian critical view; includes some fairly reliable historical material.

JESSE, EDWARD.*Favorite Haunts and Rural Studies; Including Visits to Spots of Interest in the Vicinity of Windsor and Eton.* London: John Murray, 1847. Comments on visits to Waller's erstwhile estates.

JOHNSON, SAMUEL. "Waller." *Lives of the English Poets.* Edited by G. B. Hill. Oxford: Clarendon Press, 1905, I, 249–300. Johnson is enthusiastic about neither Waller's career nor his poetry; contains nonetheless the usual telling Johnsonian perceptions.

JUDKINS, DAVID C. "Recent Studies in the Cavalier Poets: Thomas Carew, Richard Lovelace, John Suckling, and Edmund Waller." *English Literary Renaissance,* 7 (1977), 243–58. Pages 255–58 furnish an annotated bibliography of studies on Waller, comments on "canon and text," and other information. His view of Thorn-Drury's edition should be compared to Note 7, Chapter 2, above.

KORSHIN, PAUL J. "The Evolution of Neoclassical Poetics: Cleveland, Denham, and Waller as Poetic Theorists." *Eighteenth-Century Studies,* 2 (1968), 102–37. An elaborate study including the claim that Waller's contribution was "elegance."

LEAVIS, F. R. *Revaluation: Tradition and Development in English Poetry.* 1936; repr. New York: Stewart, 1947. The most significant modern dismissal of Waller.

MINER, EARL. *The Cavalier Mode from Jonson to Cotton.* Princeton: Princeton University Press, 1971. An elegant appreciation of the Cavaliers, with sensitive readings of several of Waller's poems.

NEVO, RUTH. *The Dial of Virtue: A Study of Poems on Affairs of State in the Seventeenth Century.* Princeton: Princeton University Press, 1963. Relates Waller to a tradition of political writing.

O HERIR, BRENDAN. *Expans'd Hieroglyphicks: A Critical Edition of Sir John Denham's Coopers Hill.* Berkeley and Los Angeles: University of California Press, 1969. The appendix includes an annotated printing of Waller's "Upon His Majesties Repairing of Pauls." Otherwise instructive in method of understanding poetry of the mid–1600s.

——. Review of Warren O. Chernaik's *The Poetry of Limitation.*

Modern Philology, 68 (1970-71), 100-04. Detailed and censorious comment on several problems in Waller studies.

PIPER, WILLIAM B. *The Heroic Couplet*. Cleveland and London: The Press of Case Western Reserve University, 1969. Analyzes mainly poems of flattery and illustrates Waller's "metrical short-windedness"; influenced by F. R. Leavis's denigration of Waller's "Good Form."

RICHMOND, H. M. "The Fate of Edmund Waller." *South Atlantic Quarterly*, 60 (1961), 230-38. An ingenious brief for Waller's significance; brilliant readings of several poems.

———. *The School of Love: The Evolution of the Stuart Love Lyric*. Princeton: Princeton University Press, 1964. Demonstrates Waller's significance in the tradition of European love poetry; a wide-ranging and provocative book by a scholar who is, in a casual and sophisticated way, Waller's best modern exponent.

ROECKERATH, NETTY. *Der Nachruhm Herricks and Wallers*. Leipzig: Tauchnitz; London: Williams and Norgate, 1931. A pedestrian study. Gives a short bibliography of critical opinion from 1640 to 1926.

STEELE, JAMES ARTHUR. "A Biography of Edmund Waller." Unpublished diss. University of London, 1965. A long, detailed, rambling account of Waller's life, with a wealth of valuable annotation.

STOCKDALE, PERCIVAL. "The Life of Edmund Waller." *The Works of Edmund Waller*. London: T. Davies, 1772. Perhaps too much a defense of Waller's life.

TERHUNE, FRANCES W. "A Critical Edition, with Introduction, of Edmund Waller's Alteration of Beaumont and Fletcher's *The Maid's Tragedy*." Unpublished diss. University of Florida, 1976. A critical edition of the last act of the play; presents the 1705 edition as a text revised by Waller; relates Waller's changes to political and literary history.

T[HORN-]D[RURY,] G. "Edmund Waller." *Dictionary of National Biography*. Lists at the end of the article, in abbreviated form, a number of primary and secondary sources.

———. .Manuscript notebooks. Bodley MS. Eng. Misc. d. 347. Notes taken from historical documents; includes a letter from C. H. Firth regarding sources for Waller's biography.

WALLERSTEIN, RUTH D. "The Development of the Rhetoric and Metre of the Heroic Couplet, Especially in 1625-1645." *Publications of the Modern Language Association*, 50 (1935), 166-209. Covers earlier writers from 1597. An especially persuasive and authoritative study.

WEDGWOOD, C. V. *Poetry and Politics Under the Stuarts*. Cambridge: Cambridge University Press, 1960. A study of the problems and possibilities created for poets by the Stuarts.

WERLEIN, SHEPARD H., Jr. "Edmund Waller: A Study of His Life and

Works." Unpublished diss. Harvard University, 1919. Originally a study of purported French influence (for which little evidence was found), broadened as the title indicates.

WIKELUND, P. R. "Edmund Waller's Fitt of Versifying: Deductions from a Holograph Fragment, Folger MS. X. d. 309." *Philological Quarterly*, 49 (1970), 70n and 74n. Gives a partial list of manuscript letters; promises publication of "a bibliography of Waller manuscripts."

WILLIAMSON, GEORGE. *The Proper Wit of Poetry*. London: University of Chicago Press, 1961. Places Waller and others in context of seventeenth-century wit and rhetoric.

———. "The Rhetorical Pattern of Neo-classical Wit." *Modern Philology*, 33 (1935), 55–81. A study of rhetorical development in which Waller played an important role.

Index

157

DATE DUE

ILL# 6295785	
due 3-9-85